Prestel Museum Guide

Prestel Museum Guide

Stiftung
Schleswig-Holsteinische Landesmuseen
Schloss Gottorf

Edited by
Herwig Guratzsch

Prestel
Munich · London · New York

Photographic Acknowledgments: p. 191

Front cover: Palace Island viewed from the south
Page 2: West wing facade viewed from the courtyard
Pages 6–7: Palace Island viewed from the south
Back cover: Hercules fighting the Hydra, replica of a Baroque sculpture (see p. 41)

Edited by Herwig Guratzsch
Content editor: Margret Schütte

Ground plans, site plans and genealogical tree by Monika Grade

Die Deutsche Bibliothek – CIP Einheitsaufnahme and the Library of Congress Cataloguing-in-Publication data are available

Prestel Verlag
Mandlstrasse 26, 80802 Munich
Tel. +49 (0)89-381709-0,
Fax +49 (0)89-381709-35

4 Bloomsbury Place, London WC1A 2QA
Tel. +44 (0)20 7323 5004,
Fax +44 (0)20 7636 8004

175 Fifth Avenue, Suite 402, New York,
New York 10010
Tel. +1 (212) 995-2720,
Fax +1 (212) 995-2733

www.prestel.com

Editorial direction by Curt Holtz
Copyedited by Michele Schons, Munich
Translated from the German by
John W. Gabriel, Worpswede, and
Almuth Seebohm, Munich

Design and typography: Kluy & Kluy
Lithography: LVD, Berlin
Printing and binding: Passavia Druckservice GmbH, Passau

Printed in Germany on acid-free paper

ISBN 3-7913-2574-4 (English edition)
ISBN 3-7913-2555-8 (German edition)
ISBN 3-7913-2568-x (Danish edition)

STIFTUNG SCHLESWIG-HOLSTEINISCHE
LANDESMUSEEN SCHLOSS GOTTORF

Stiftung Schleswig-Holsteinische Landesmuseen Schloss Gottorf
24837 Schleswig

info@schloss-gottorf.de
www.schloss-gottorf.de

Opening Hours

April–October
daily 10 am–6 pm

November–March
Tuesday–Friday 10 am–4 pm
Saturday–Sunday 10 am–5 pm
closed Mondays

Guided tours for school groups begin at 9 am

Educational Center/Bookshop
Tel. +49 (0)4621-81 32 33
Fax +49 (0)4621-81 35 55

How to get there:
By train (15-min. walk from the train station)
By bus (2, 3, 4)
By car: take the A7,
Jagel exit if coming from Hamburg (5 min.),
Schuby exit if coming from Flensburg (5 min.)

Contents

Contributors

UB	Ursula Bode
KB	Klaus Bokelmann
BB	Bernd Bünsche
JD	Jan Drees
UD	Ute Drews
MF	Mechtild Freudenberg
TG	Thomas Gädeke
MG	Michael Gebühr
HG	Herwig Guratzsch
CK	Claudia Kanowski
BK	Bettina Kess
UK	Uta Kuhl
HM	Heinrich Mehl
TP	Thomas Pöpper
CR	Christian Radtke
BR	Britta Reimann
MS	Margret Schütte

Gottorf Palace: The Largest Museum Complex in Northern Germany

For anyone who imagines Germany's northern border running just above Hamburg, Gottorf Palace is bound to be an unknown quantity, for it lies some 60 miles north of the Hanseatic city, in the state of Schleswig-Holstein, an attractive, narrow strip of land between the North and Baltic Seas that borders on Denmark. Its most striking feature is the Schlei, a body of water that extends far inland, like a finger of the sea. Toward the end lies the city of Schleswig, and the massive Baroque palace surrounded by water. Centuries ago a highly important military bastion, Gottorf lost its strategic significance and, between 1850 and 1950, gradually fell into disrepair. Anyone who has visited the magnificent edifice in the past twenty years may find it difficult to imagine that it was once a rundown barracks.

Gottorf Palace is the largest museum complex in northern Germany. It is the headquarters of Schleswig-Holstein's State Museums, which were united to form an independent foundation in 1999. The extensive collections on display, storerooms, laboratories and workshops occupy a total area of approximately 600,000 square feet—five times that of the Alte Pinakothek in Munich. Not that sheer size is any measure of a museum's quality, of course. The notion of an overwhelming number of exhibits may tend to discourage more than encourage potential visitors.

In fact, the veritably inexhaustible artistic and cultural, archaeological and ethnological heritage present at Gottorf and its branches is probably the most challenging and exciting problem facing the 130 foundation staff members in their effort to present this variety to the public. Yet if they thought the task impossible, they would have no motivation to tackle it. They know that visitors come not to be overwhelmed, but to look, learn and enjoy. Class, not mass, is the point of the enterprise.

This is why the present museum guide is not of kaleidoscopic breadth, bringing thousands of objects into simultaneous, if confusing, focus. Instead, it presents a selection of beautiful and inspiring pieces in homeopathic doses, as it were. This narrowing down of the collections to key examples opens windows on entire departments. *Pars pro toto* is the underlying idea. And it is reflected not only in this publication, which can do no more than suggest the richness of the Schleswig-Holstein State Museums, but in the actual presentation at Gottorf Palace and its affiliated facilities. Each individual object is given space in which to unfold, enabling visitors and readers to stand back, concentrate and feel the fascination of great and unique creations by human hands.

As we all know from experience, the rush and abundance of superficial visual impressions that bombard us every day can lead to nervousness, irritation and unease. Museums, in contrast, offer the chance to concentrate on true testimonies of culture—unusual, unique and incomparable—or, in the case of folk art and ethnological specimens, to view those typical and characteristic things that shed light on the history of a people and help us define our own position in relation to it.

The plethora of displays at Gottorf Palace, reflected in the selection of exhibits discussed in the present guidebook, crystallizes into sharp contours, revealing contexts and cross-relationships. We begin with the cogent presentation in the four wings of the palace proper, and a visit to the Gallery of Classical Modernism, which includes the Horn, Tappert and Wimmer foundations as well as portions of the Heckel Estate at Hemmenhofen and loans from the Rauert Collection. This is followed by the Kreuzstall, a historic riding stable now devoted to temporary exhibitions of twentieth-century art and special exhibitions on past and contemporary trends.

Then we take a "Historical Tour" through art, cultural history and the early stages of human evolution as revealed by archaeology. After continuing to Nydam Hall, with its fascinating warship dating from A.D. 320, we proceed to the Wikinger Museum Haithabu.

After looking at the large collection of historic carriages on Palace Island, we turn to the permanent local history collections on Hesterberg in Schleswig, which is supplemented by related temporary exhibitions. The tour is rounded off by a trip to the Museum of Cast Iron in Büdelsdorf, the Jewish Museum in Rendsburg and to Cismar Monastery, located outside Schleswig, north of Lübeck,

Design for a new Globe House, by architects Hilmer & Sattler

Gottorf Palace viewed from the south

which is home to, among other things, projects exploring the links between visual art and literature (relying in part on connections with the "Weisses Haus," the literature center in Cismar).

Museums are ubiquitous in today's world, and specialization is the rule. But museum associations covering a diverse range of fields that inspire interdisciplinary insights and encourage the discovery of cross-references are rare. The strength of Gottorf Palace lies precisely in its astonishing complexity and diversity. *HG*

The History of Schleswig-Holstein's State Museums

Both Schleswig-Holstein State Museums, of Art and Cultural History and of Archaeology, moved into Gottorf Palace in 1947, when it was still in an extreme state of disrepair. Originally located in Kiel, the museums had developed into independent institutions by the middle of the nineteenth century. The year 1835 marked the founding of the "Museum Vaterländischer Alterthümer," or Museum of

Gottorf Palace viewed from the west

National Antiquities, whose name and venue subsequently changed several times. Associated from 1873 with the Christian Albrecht University, the museum underwent a long and systematic expansion until, in 1999, it left the university to become part of a foundation. Under the name of State Archaeological Museum, it was affiliated with the State Museum of Art and Cultural History.

Also established in Kiel, in 1875, was a museum that focused on the cultural history of Schleswig-Holstein. The Thaulow Museum collected ecclesiastical and decorative art, as well as folk art items. A key concern was to familiarize artisans of the day with the high artistic standards set by previous generations. In other words, it was a

museum with an educational function, and only gradually did it begin to arrange its collections according to historical criteria, presenting them in their proper art historical contexts. Prior to World War II, the Thaulow Museum had been renamed the Schleswig-Holstein State Museum, and subsequently began to link the art and cultural history of northern Germany, beyond redrawn national frontiers, with that of its neighbor Denmark and beyond.

When the fledgling postwar government of Schleswig-Holstein shifted its seat from Schleswig to Kiel, the two state museums, together with the Kiel State Archive, were united in Schleswig at Gottorf Palace. The Gottorf museum complex with affiliated institutions opened its doors in 1950. Karl Kersten, Director of the State Archaeological Museum, and Ernst Schlee, Director of the Museum of Art and Cultural History, faced a daunting task. They had somehow to incorporate their collections in a venerable but outmoded building, much of whose historical architecture had been strongly disfigured. What's more, the collections had little in common with the original palace furnishings and therefore clashed with their surroundings. The challenge was to create a fruitful dialogue between content and shell, between highly diverse exhibits and historical architecture.

Schlee, who also assumed responsibility for maintaining the palace as a historical monument, succeeded in credibly integrating

Cismar Monastery viewed from the southwest

Wikinger Museum Haithabu viewed from the north

the displays and their message in the existing rooms. He also oversaw the restoration of the original interiors of historically significant rooms, such as the Gothic Hall and Deer Hall (Hirschsaal). With an eye to modern needs, Schlee proceeded on two basic premises. First, there would be a Historical Tour, which would link Gothic Hall, Deer Hall and Chapel, among the few authentic legacies of the ducal period in its heyday. Second, despite Schlee's personal focus on crafts, the collection would be expanded to include the fine arts.

Schlee's successors continued to pursue these two lines of development with imagination and enthusiasm. War losses incurred in the outstanding ducal art collections of the seventeenth century were compensated by the acquisition of suitable pieces, and a link was established across the centuries, with topics ranging from local history to twentieth-century art.

At the State Archaeological Museum, an increasing focus on basic research began in collaboration with the University and the State Bureau of Archaeology (Landesamt für Archäologie). The availability of outside funding, especially from the German Research Association (Deutsche Forschungsgemeinschaft), led to remarkable progress in both the scholarly and museum fields, including the foundation of the Wikinger Museum Haithabu in 1985.

Since 1999, under the aegis of the foundation, the two museums and their branches have improved their efficiency by undertaking joint projects and consolidating certain working areas. Increasing financial independence has given the museums an opportunity to supplement efficient museum design by a reconstruction of the devastated historical grounds. Thanks to generous private aid, restoration work has begun on the celebrated Baroque Garden and the seventeenth-century Giant Globe, which has been exceptionally well received. None of this progress would have been possible without the efforts of the foundation.

An idea of the Baroque splendor of the ducal era can be conveyed to today's visitors, at least as far as external appearances go. This sadly cannot be said of the way of life and everyday reality of that period, or of such lost treasures as the renowned seventeenth-century *Kunstkammer*, or Cabinet of Curiosities, and the remarkable ducal library. Nor could any virtual simulation of the role played by this magnificent palace since the twelfth century—initially as a bishop's seat, then as a ducal seat—hope to do it justice. What we can do is ask questions about the history of Schleswig-Holstein in light of the many-facetted works of art now present at Gottorf. This will increasingly be the aim of the foundation's work. As unlikely as the marriage between the State Museums and the old palace may seem, it has proven eminently fruitful and stimulating to the awareness of younger generations, providing an experience of identity and local heritage that helps them define their own future. *HG*

Art and Cultural History

Sculpture: From the Middle Ages to the Present

Our rich and diverse collection of regional ecclesiastical art is located in the main building of the palace, in a room known as the Gothic Hall. This is the loveliest secular Gothic interior in Schleswig-Holstein. The architecture is in a late-Gothic style, verging on that of the Renaissance. Its ribbed vaults still bear traces of the original red paint scheme and gilded laurel design. The room provides an ideal setting for the collection of sacred sculpture.

From the year 1667 onward, under Duke Christian Albert, the Gothic Hall served as the Gottorf Library. This former use is still reflected in the fragmentary signs of the zodiac seen on some of the arch spandrels, which provided orientation to the library sections.

In 1875, a number of "Christian antiquities" were brought down from church attics and storerooms, and saved from certain decay by Professor Gustav Thaulow of Kiel. These formed the nucleus of a collection of ecclesiastical sculptures and handcrafted objects at the Kiel museum named after Thaulow, and subsequently of the present collection of medieval to contemporary art in the Schleswig-Holstein State Museums Foundation.

The impression of the Gothic Hall is determined by a variety of individual figures, which originally served as devotional images.

*Schleswig master, **Crucifixion**, ca. 1250, Kosel, oak, Crucifix: 52 x 50 x 6 ¾ in., Virgin: 47 ¼ x 12 ¼ x 11 in., St. John: 44 ⅞ x 11 x 7 ⅞ in.*

These include depictions of the seated Virgin and Archangel Michael, and small sculptural groups, such as that of St. George and the Dragon, and of the king's daughter, usually depicted kneeling. These devotionals, private or public, had an emotional emphasis that reflected a new, personal faith, and the need for figures of identification. An even more prominent place in the collection is held by a series of altarpieces from various Schleswig-Holstein churches, which vividly illustrate the development of wood sculpture from the late Romanesque to the late Gothic period.

The earliest wood sculptures found in the region date back to the early thirteenth century, when churches built in stone began to be furnished with elaborate paintings, sculptures and altarpieces. Their central feature was often a Crucifixion group. Placed on a beam at the height of the arch abutment in the choir or suspended from chains, such images were the focus of the congregation's worship. A group of this kind from Kosel, a small village in the Schleswig region of Schwansen, dates from about 1250. It stands near the entrance to the Gothic Hall, on an oak replica of the original choir beam.

Depicting Christ on the Cross flanked by the mourning Virgin and St. John, the work reveals stylistic affinities with portal figures of the French High Gothic, such as those at Amiens and Reims cathedrals. Characteristic features are the cascading folds of the drapery, the broad planes of the faces and the corporeal volumes of the figures. The Kosel Crucifixion marks the inception of a new, French-inspired sculptural style in the Dukedom of Schleswig. This gives the piece a special place in the collection, despite its incomplete state of preservation and lack of original polychrome finish.

Owing to its imposing size and extremely fine original finish, the Landkirchen Retable (ca. 1380), from St. Peter's Church in Landkirchen on Fehmarn Island, is among the most outstanding specimens in the medieval sculpture collection. This two-wing oak altarpiece—whose original painting on the outside of the wings is not preserved—has multiple-figure reliefs in the central section and wings representing scenes from the Passion and the Apotheosis of Christ. Owing to the planar, abbreviated style of the figures, it is sometimes difficult to say exactly what actions they are performing.

The center of the retable originally contained depictions of the Last Judgment and a Crucifixion, which, like one of the reliefs on the right wing, have been lost. Clear links obviously exist between this piece and the Lettner Retable (ca. 1370) at the Monastery Church in Bad Doberan, Mecklenburg-Vorpommern, which is considered the oldest retable with figurative scenes, as well as the Grabow Altarpiece from St. Peter's in Hamburg, created by Master Bertram about 1380 (now in the Hamburg Kunsthalle). The extensive use of gold and silver leaf, and the colored ornamentation and lusterwork on the reliefs of the Landkirchen Retable, for the most

Circle of Master Bertram of Minden, ***Landkirchen Retable, The Lamentation,*** *ca. 1380, oak, 74 3/4 x 214 1/8 x 5 1/8 in.*

part still original, show all the variety and splendor of late fourteenth-century finishing techniques.

Dating from about the same period as the Landkirchen Retable, but much more reserved in effect, are the finely carved alabaster reliefs from an altarpiece (ca. 1400) that originated in Nottingham, England. Presumably ordered by a Lübeck tradesman at the London Steelyard, they later came from the Hanseatic League city to the church at Gross-Grönau.

Alabaster, a fine-grained, easily worked variety of gypsum, first came into use in England. Deposits discovered near Nottingham encouraged a burgeoning production of statuettes, reliefs and altarpieces, which, thanks not least to the commerce of the Hanseatic League, were distributed throughout Europe. The reliefs in the Gottorf collection exhibit not only skilled carving but a very subtle polychrome decor. Although several of the five pieces are in a fragmentary state, we can detect scenes from the Life of the Virgin, with the Trinity in the center. In contrast to those of the Landkirchen Retable, these small, emotionally rendered scenes convey an intimate mood.

A similar effect is seen in the slightly inclined head of high artistic quality that once belonged to a limestone statue of the Virgin (ca.

1420–30). Her gentle smile was probably meant for the infant Jesus resting in her arms. The work of a Lübeck master, the figure with its charming and touching features was a devotional image, whose emotion and beauty were intended to convey a religious message in a direct, undogmatic way. The head was discovered during excavations of the former Bridgettine Convent of Marienwohld, near Lauenburg, which was dissolved in 1588. Apparently the figure originally had a colored finish; the holes in the crown enabled the attachment of applications of the kind found on Madonnas of the same period in Bohemia and southern Germany.

One of the major Low German carvers of the first quarter of the sixteenth century was Hans Brüggemann. His best-known work, the Bordesholm Retable (1520) in Schleswig Cathedral, a monumental piece whose motifs combine blunt realism of detail with a profound spirituality, bears outstanding witness to the emergent art of the Renaissance. The typical traits of Brüggemann's carvings, only a few of which survive, include a reliance on the effect of unpainted wood. This was also characteristic of nearly all the works of the celebrated Tilman Riemenschneider, who was concurrently active in southern Germany.

With the Goschhof Retable (ca. 1512–17), the State Museum of Art and Cultural History possesses the earliest work ascribed to Brüggemann. In the shrine we see a depiction of the Holy Family (apart from the lost Infant Jesus) and a very rare representation of the Tiburtine Sibyl, who is showing Emperor Augustus the vision of the

Lübeck master, ***Head of the Virgin,*** *fragment of a sculpture, ca. 1420–30, former Bridgettine Convent, Marienwohld near Lauenburg, 5 5/8 x 4 7/8 x 4 1/8 in.*

Goschhof Retable, ca. 1512–17, oak, 83 ½ x 120 ½ x 15 in.

Christ Child sitting in a tree. The predella contains a depiction of the Fourteen Holy Helpers. The superstructure of the shrine, where we must imagine God the Father with the Dove of the Holy Spirit, is missing.

Installed on the grounds of Palace Island are a number of sculptures that date from the late nineteenth century to our own day. The trees and shrubbery, changing with the seasons and continually modulating the light, form a lovely setting for the largest sculpture park in northern Germany.

One of the leading German sculptors of the turn of the century, Adolf Brütt (1855–1939) of Husum, is represented here with his major work *Eve with Her Children* (1889). This life-size bronze shows typical traits of late nineteenth-century art on the verge of Art Nouveau, in forms that are both sensual and maternal. Deep in thought, Eve, the first mother, strides forward, in her left arm little Cain, his arm around her neck and looking back over her shoulder, and in her right the sleeping Abel. According to the sculptor, the figure of a woman with her two children represents the mother of mankind, who accepted the enormous responsibility of giving birth to the first, and already antagonistic, brothers. She symbolizes Mother Nature, who both gives and takes away.

Prime among the many sculptures by Ernst Barlach in the Horn Foundation is his monumental and starkly expressive *Hovering Man.* The original was created in 1927 as a memorial for the dead of World

*Adolf Brütt (1855–1939), **Eve with Her Children**, 1889, bronze, 66 ½ x 26 ¾ x 14 ½ in.*

War I and installed in Güstrow Cathedral. It was subsequently destroyed by the Nazis.

The present version is one of three existing posthumous bronze casts. The only version to be cast from the original plaster, at the behest of Barlach's friends in 1939, is now in the Antonite Church, Cologne (the plaster was destroyed in 1944 at the Noack Foundry, Berlin). In 1951, Noack took a mold from this first posthumous casting, which was used for the version that returned to Güstrow in 1952 and for the Gottorf version in 1987. Barlach created memorials to the war dead for Güstrow, Kiel, Magdeburg and Hamburg; the present sculpture represents the first of the four. *Hovering Man* is viewed as one of the most unusual pictorial inventions of the twentieth century. The motif of hovering in meditative calm is evoked with a compellingness quite unparalleled in European sculpture. Barlach sought to penetrate the truth of the human condition, and depicted his findings not only in the medium of sculpture but in prints and literature as well. The face of *Hovering Man* definitely bears the features of Käthe Kollwitz—unintentionally, as Barlach said, but still a clear sign of his close relationship with and admiration for his woman fellow-artist.

Purposely installed immediately behind Barlach's sculpture is a figure frieze by Gerhard Marcks. Created in 1947, the just over life-size figures of fired, dark-brown terracotta supplement a project entrusted to Barlach in 1930 by Carl Georg Heise, director of the Lübeck Museum. In 1933 the Nazis prevented the completion and installation of the piece, titled *Community of Saints*, of which Barlach had finished three figures. Marcks created six further figures, which, together with Barlach's three, were installed in 1949 on the west facade of St. Catherine's in Lübeck. Deeply affected by the Nazi reign of terror and war, Marcks infused the figures with suffering and sorrow, and even included the "Incendiary" at the far left edge, who embodies the principle of evil and human malice. Pain and despair are transmuted into a resigned tranquillity, seemingly reflecting the mental situation in which the people of this country, perpetrators and victims alike, were ensnared for twelve years. Quite near Marcks's frieze, we come upon a series of tall, slender sculptures in a strikingly expressive style by Jan Koblasa.

Born in Bohemia in 1932, Koblasa left former Czechoslovakia in 1968, after the ominous end of the Spring of Prague. Since then he has lived and worked in Schleswig-Holstein. The experience of persecution and emigration influenced Koblasa's art much as Nazism did that of Barlach and Marcks. This is reflected in a wide range of sculptures, paintings and prints, which, like those of Koblasa's two great predecessors, are distinctly religious in thrust. His St. Sebastian, a martyr of the latter half of the third century

Gerhard Marcks (1889–1981), ***Figure Frieze for the West Facade of St. Catherine's in Lübeck, Incendiary,*** *1947, terracotta, 82 ⅝ x 19 ¼ x 10 ⅝ in., Kulturring der Studien- und Fördergesellschaft der Schleswig-Holsteinischen Wirtschaft*

Jan Koblasa (b. 1932), ***St. Sebastian,*** *1991, bronze, 157 1/2 x 35 3/8 x 35 3/8 in., Rolf Horn Foundation*

who has come to personify torment and martyrdom like no other, expresses the sufferings endured by the victims of Communist dictatorship. The sculpture stands outside the exhibition building, near four other Koblasa pieces. These likewise have an anthropomorphic, if enigmatically abbreviated form that evokes messengers from another, transcendent realm. These figures correspond with two further messengers inside the building. At this point, a window provides a view over the entire collection of sculptures, against the backdrop of the park.

Also located in the sculpture park is Bernhard Heiliger's (1915–1995) space-defining iron sculpture *Tree between Two Worlds* of 1982 (see p. 81). Its angular configuration and interplay of solid volumes with negative spaces represent another key current in late twentieth-century sculpture. The piece seems to anticipate the growing threat posed to nature by human activities of every kind. It metaphorically suggests the tensions between stability and precariousness, earthbound and hovering, open and closed form. The spherical shape, characteristic of Heiliger's work, evokes an uneasy relationship between earth and heaven. A smooth, closed version of the sphere featured frequently in the artist's steel sculptures after 1980. For Heiliger, its consummate form represented an aspect of the inexhaustible creative forces of nature, but was also a simile for the divine harmony of the cosmos. While Heiliger's sculptures do not deny the physical properties of steel, their elements seem to defy gravity, enabling them to convey transcendent, universal meanings. Sweeping, open forms are the prime features of Heiliger's formal idiom. Both animate and inanimate matter are part of the whole, the universe—

this was his fundamental premise. Until his death, Heiliger endeavored to bridge the steadily widening gap between technology and nature. *BB*

Art of the Baroque Period: A Feast for the Eyes

Apart from its inglorious use as a barracks in the nineteenth century, Gottorf Palace—and with it the conception of the State Museum of Art and Cultural History collections—was shaped by the Baroque period like no other. Gottorf's heyday, which saw the emergence of the remarkable northern German versions of late Renaissance and High Baroque, lasted for a good century and a half. Beginning with the appointment in 1544 of Duke Adolf to the position of first Duke of Schleswig-Holstein-Gottorf, it continued beyond the death of Frederick IV in 1702, until the seizure of the Gottorf fief by the Danish crown in 1713. The residence of the Dukes of Gottorf on Palace Island in the Schlei was considerably expanded, yet still remained modest compared to other German princely courts. Gottorf attained renown as a northern European cultural center that far exceeded its actual political significance.

The items on display in this department of the museum—which includes an outstanding variety of sculptures, paintings, furniture, tapestries and Gobelins, books and decorative art—record this heyday. A theatrical presence, a love of ostentation and the grand gesture that in the post-postmodern view is often mistaken for mere bombast; a use of dazzling *trompe-l'œil* effects to stimulate the senses and emotions both rhetorically and physically—thus one might roughly describe the nature and range of the artistic means of the Baroque.

The derivation of the word "baroque" is interesting. The term originated in the Romance languages. In Portuguese it initially had the specific connotation of "oblong" or "irregular" (as with pearls), and later took on the more general meaning of "against the rules," "odd" or "not in good taste." In French, around the middle of the eighteenth century, the term was applied to architecture that did not conform to neoclassical decorum. A century later, in Germany, the adjective "barock" came to be used in connection with other genres of art, without its previously pejorative implications. In other words, the use of "baroque" to describe a style and era dates no further back than the nascent interest of art historians in that period.

Unlike the rational art of the Renaissance, which was devoted to truth to nature, commensurability and regularity, the "irrational" art—as our brief outline of the term "baroque" indicates—of the immediately preceding century, with its direct appeal to the senses and emotions, was more attractive to people of the eighteenth century. The means employed with more or less skill by Baroque artists served not only to display their own virtuosity but to pursue higher aims, such as conveying transcendent content of a religious, mythical or historical nature. Charged with such meaning, Baroque works not rarely also bolstered the status of the absolutist rulers who ordered them, reflecting their power through persuasive visual splendor.

Purposes of this kind were served, for instance, by the large wall hangings with elaborate floral and fruit borders made at the Royal

*Aubusson manufactory, **Triumph of Alexander**, one of a cycle of four tapestries, ca. 1670, provenance: Damp estate, Schwansen, wool, silk, 116 ⅛ x 161 ⅜ in.*

Anonymous 16th- or 17th-century Flemish master (?), ***Picture Puzzle Landscape*** *(horizontally) or* ***Profile of a Bearded Man*** *(vertically), oil on panel, 5 ½ x 8 ¼ in.*

Aubusson manufactory in France about 1670. Woven in a technique known as *basselisse*, they were very probably intended for the Estate of Damp, on the Baltic coast in the Schwansen region of Schleswig-Holstein. Originally belonging to a cycle of four, the tapestries depict—or rather, glorify—the deeds of Alexander the Great (356–323 B.C.), the ruler and hero who unified Orient and Occident. We see his encounter with Roxane, the thirteen-year-old daughter of a Bactrian prince, whose extraordinary beauty was praised by the authors of antiquity, and Alexander's triumphant entry into a city as commander after a victorious battle.

Let us look more closely at this latter tapestry. The scene, spread over a good 130-square-foot area, swarms with figures and attributes. Crowned with laurel, the ruler over the known world rides majestically in a quadriga through a city whose power is symbolized by colonnades, accompanied by musicians playing trumpets, flutes and harps, a guard of charioteers in short Roman cloaks and various foot soldiers. In the hall of the mansion at Damp where it originally hung, the horizontal composition must have had the effect of a window on ancient history. It employs a popular device of the period—figures such as the man seen from behind, who opens the scene on the left are overlapped by the border. This not only underscores the window-like character of the scene and suggests that the viewer is eye-witness to the distant event, but evokes the presence of a long triumphal train continuing beyond the frame. It is tempting to imagine the lord of the estate standing with his family and friends before this ingenious window onto the past, sunning himself in the light of Alexander at the zenith of his glory.

Besides such apotheoses, another typical characteristic of the Baroque era was a striving for knowledge of nature and the universe, which had continued unbroken since the rediscovery of antiquity in the Renaissance. This was reflected in an interest in scientific instruments, which was particularly strong in the case of Duke Frederick III of Gottorf (1597–1659). Apart from erecting what was probably the most astonishing apparatus of the northern German Baroque, the giant terrestrial and celestial globe in the terrace garden (see pp. 39–44), Frederick III established the rich collection of the Gottorf *Kunstkammer* (*Cabinet of Curiosities*). Expanded into a veritable "mirror of the world" by court scholar Adam Olearius (1599–1671)—born as Adam Oehlschlaegel in Aschersleben—who brought back a variety of artworks, objects and curiosities from expeditions to Russia and Persia, this *Wunderkammer* had taken on a truly universal

Bendix Grodtschilling the Elder and the Younger (ca. 1620–1690; 1655–1707), ***Picture Puzzle of King Christian V of Denmark****, 1685, oil on panel (in the original, partly gilt frame), 33 ⅞ x 22 ½ in.*

character by the seventeenth century. The duke was a passionate collector of optical and mathematical instruments, as well as picture puzzles, which, with the help of mirrors and lenses, playfully and artfully demonstrated the laws of perspective and light refraction.

In addition to mathematically constructed perspective views of fantastic architecture, this genre includes a trick portrait, or picture puzzle, of King Christian V, dating from 1685 and acquired in 1980 (formerly Royal Danish Cabinet of Curiosities, Copenhagen). The work is ascribed to Bendix Grodtschilling the Elder and the Younger, a father and son team active at the Copenhagen court. Strangely, although the monogram "C5" at the top of the frame refers to Christian V, we look in vain for his likeness in the painting. Instead, the middle of the panel contains a depiction of his mother, Queen Sophie Amalie (1628–1685), closely surrounded by a circle of no less than eight royal ancestors of the House of Oldenburg. But where is the reigning monarch? When we look through the lens of an ocular, in which prisms produce a portrait of Christian V from segments of the eight portraits in the circle, his image appears within the proverbial split-second in place of his mother. As we know from historical sources, a very similar optical instrument, once in the Gottorf *Kunstkammer* but since lost, showed—or, rather, conjured—a portrait of Duke Frederick III.

The little apparatus consisting of a painstakingly rendered panel, finely carved frame and optical instrument represented more than a sophisticated courtly amusement and a modern scientific demonstration. It might have been a melancholy metaphor of the entire period. As if under a microscope, a deeper layer of the Baroque mind comes into view. Distinguished by royal rank, intellectual curiosity, wide learning and artistic sensibility, the king portrayed—or not portrayed—presents himself as shaped by, indeed literally composed of, many factors, illustrated by the dominant, lasting features of his dynastic origins. He himself appears merely as an ephemeral inhabitant of the earth. Christian V, the mighty monarch, lives for a historically brief moment, from one blink of an eye to the next. His personal presence seems limited to the time an equally ephemeral viewer sees him through the lens. Like his idol, Alexander the Great, Christian V may have suspected that he would survive in the eyes of posterity only through his deeds, especially his famous ones.

There could hardly be any more concentrated and subtle embodiment of scientific insight and courtly representation, paired with their refraction in an awareness of the transitoriness of earthly existence and glory—*vanitas*—than in a seemingly so playful and amusing chamber piece like our picture puzzle.

The vanitas theme more or less strongly infuses many of the works of art in the Gottorf Baroque Gallery, in which, apart from northern German and Italian painting, Netherlandish art holds a prominent place. Individual and group portraits, still lifes, landscapes, religious and allegorical subjects were already present at Gottorf in great numbers in the seventeenth century, when its multifarious relations with the Netherlands were at a peak.

We feel especially fortunate to be able to present Baroque art in a contemporaneous suite of rooms in the north wing, whose stuccowork dates from after 1624. Formerly part of the apartments of Duke Frederick III, these rooms are among the best preserved in the palace. Although their Gobelins and tapestries, wall coverings of leather decorated with gold and silver leaf, or of Safavid, or Persian, silk brought here by the 1640 expedition, have not survived or have been in part replaced by similar pieces, the Baroque Department's outstanding works convey a good idea of the erstwhile splendor of the palace furnishings. *TP*

Karel Dujardin (ca. 1622–1678), ***Homo bulla: Child Blowing Soap Bubbles as an Allegory of Transience,*** *oil on canvas, 45 1/4 x 34 5/8 in.*

Frederick III and His Court Artist: Three Works by Jürgen Ovens

Thanks to his skilled conduct of family affairs, marrying his daughter to the young Swedish King Charles X Gustav, Duke Frederick III of Schleswig-Holstein-Gottorf (1597–1659) attained sovereignty for his dukedom in the face of continual demands on the part of the related Danish royal house. This went hand in hand with his efforts, building on the achievements of his ancestors, to make Gottorf a cultural center along the lines of other, much larger European courts. Frederick furthered the arts and sciences, brought the scholar Adam Olearius and the artist Jürgen Ovens to his court and, surely aided by his wife, Maria Elizabeth of Saxony, improved the quality of

Jürgen Ovens (1623–1678), ***Allegory of the Hereditary Succession of the Ducal House of Gottorf****, 1646, oil on oak panel, 192 ¼ x 26 ½ in., Kulturstiftung des Landes Schleswig-Holstein*

the royal chamber orchestra. The Gottorf collections gained an international reputation, and the court became an attraction both for young aristocrats on their grand tour and a range of foreign scholars.

When the duke decided to appoint a court artist, he chose Jürgen Ovens (1623–1678), a young painter from Tönning on the Eiderstedt peninsula who had trained in the Netherlands and enjoyed early success in the best circles. According to Arnold Houbraken in his 1718–21 biographical work of Netherlandish artists, *De Groote Schouburgh der Nederlantsche Konstschilderessen* (The Great Theater of Netherlandish Painters), Ovens had been a pupil of Rembrandt. All that we know for certain, however, is that he was acquainted with Rembrandt's teacher, Pieter Lastman, and occasionally painted in his manner, but generally showed a preference for Van Dyck, a few works of whose he owned. A case in point is Ovens's signed and dated painting of 1646, which is thought to be an *Allegory of the Hereditary Succession of the Ducal House of Gottorf.*

Prior to its acquisition in 1986, the painting, whose provenance can be traced no further back than the contemporary English art trade, was titled *Charity* or *Caritas.* This was a widespread theme in the premodern period, and quite frequently appeared in Ovens's work. Here he has depicted a mother holding her youngest child in her lap, surrounded by three other children of various ages. Visible in the background are another three children of about the same age. Strikingly, the mother is clad in red and blue garments, recalling those found in depictions of the Virgin. Her exquisite necklace and headdress, and elaborate shoes, are indications of high social standing. The fruit held by the youngest child, and the cornucopia with fruit, can clearly be read as symbols of fertility. The grapevine growing up the tree behind mother and child probably directly relates to the emblem of a vine-entwined elm, a popular seventeenth-century symbol of conjugal love, and also of a love that remains vital beyond death. The fact that one of the three children in the background is depicted reaching out for a tendril is surely no coincidence.

The allegorical and emblematic allusions, together with the care devoted to the rendering, strongly suggest that the work was commissioned by the duke. When we compare the figures' features with Ovens's later individual and group portraits of the duke's family, and consider the number and age of Frederick III and Maria Elizabeth's living or deceased children at the time the painting was executed, it would appear more than probable that it depicts the duchess among her surviving sons, August Frederick (in her lap), Frederick, successor to the regency (as shepherd with pipes and jar), John George (with cornucopia) and the later Duke Christian Albert. The couple's three deceased children are nonetheless included in the life of the family.

This would make the work an allegory with portrait-like characteristics, a so-called *portrait historié* so typical of the seventeenth century. And perhaps the twenty-three-year-old artist painted it while still in the Netherlands, in 1646, with an eye to obtaining an audience with his sovereign. At any rate, we do know that Ovens became Gottorf court artist in 1652.

At an auction in Copenhagen, a small oil on copper was offered as a *Portrait of a Gentleman in a Black Coat, Standing in Front of a Manor House* and attributed to Wolfgang Heimbach (ca. 1615–1678), who originated from Övelgönne near Oldenburg. Judging by remnants of a slip on the reverse, the painting had previously been in an English collection. The facial features and physique of the man depicted immediately recall Duke Frederick III of Schleswig-Holstein-Gottorf. The background confirms this supposition—the "manor house" with its onion dome is none other than Friedrichsburg, named after the duke, in Gottorf's Neuwerk Garden. This large pleasure seat in the "Persian style" was built from 1651 to 1654 to the design of court scholar Adam Olearius, and harbored, among a number of other treasures, the famous Gottorf Giant Globe, also conceived by Olearius. In front of Friedrichsburg, visible between the gentleman's stick and boot top, is a round pavilion with dome

Jürgen Ovens, ***Duke Frederick III of Schleswig-Holstein-Gottorf in Front of Neuwerk Garden at Gottorf****, second half of 1650s, oil on copper, 6 ¾ x 6 ¼ in.*

and even the stone Hercules statue that stands in the pond of the same name in Neuwerk Garden.

As far as authorship of the work is concerned, Ovens would seem more likely than Heimbach, because from 1653 to 1662, when the painting was executed, Heimbach was in the employ of the Danish royal house and no record of him exists in the Gottorf accounts. Moreover, there is a surviving sepia drawing of about the same format by Ovens, depicting the Duchess of Gottorf (Bremen Kunsthalle). In both drawing and oil painting, Frederick III stands on the bank of Hercules Pond. Judging by the position of the pavilion and statue, the vantage point of the drawing is further right than that of the painting, so that Friedrichsburg can be imagined to the right, outside the picture. In addition, there is another portrait of the duke by Ovens, likewise in oil on copper (private collection, Finland), which measures 8 ⅞ x 7 ¼ cm and dates from approximately the same period.

The first postwar director at Gottorf, Ernst Schlee, was so moved by the acquisition of the little panel in 1988 that he declared he could kiss it, because Duke Frederick III seemed a veritable personification of the Gottorf Globe.

Another painting by Ovens shows a mother and child in the foreground of a landscape of woods and lakes—perhaps a portrait of Queen Hedwig Eleonora of Sweden with her only child, the Swedish crown prince Charles. The work can be dated to the late 1650s. It is neither signed nor dated, and was unknown until its acquisition. Yet the persons represented show great similarities to a mother and child in a signed Ovens painting.

Ovens expert Gertrud Schlüter-Göttsche believes this is a portrait of the artist's wife, Maria, with their daughter Catharina, born in 1657. Yet this would seem unlikely in view of a key difference, besides the rocks in the background in that painting and the woods and lakes in the Gottorf one: the figures in the latter wear more elaborate gold and pearl jewelry, which would seem to indicate a very high social standing. And since there are no signs of an allegory, it is unlikely that the artist's wife and daughter were the sitters. Nor is it probable that a mother would be depicted in the seventeenth century with only one child when she had several—as was the case with the Ovens family. Everything speaks for an aristocratic portrait, very probably of members of the Gottorf ducal house.

The most likely candidate would be the daughter of Frederick III of Schleswig-Holstein-Gottorf, Hedwig Eleonora (1636–1715), who in 1654 married the Swedish king, Charles X Gustav (1622–1660)—an event that Ovens recorded in three paintings. The sole child of the marriage and successor to the throne, Charles XI, was born on December 4, 1655. The likeness with the portrait of Hedwig Eleonora in Ovens's *Allegory of the Coronation of Queen Hedwig Eleonora* of 1654 (Gripsholm Palace) lends this assumption a certain plausibility, even though no further similarities would support this identification. The landscape in the left background is too vague to make out the silhouette of any palace, whether Gottorf or Gripsholm. The rocky area in the second painting might well suggest a Swedish setting. But what clinches the case is the presence in the mother's and child's garments of the old Swedish national colors, blue and yellow, which were worn into battle by the legendary King Gustavus II Adolphus, the "Hero of Midnight." This unusual color combination is determinant, in a figurative sense. The royal identification also explains why the little prince wears a golden ornament mounted with a pearl in his hair, and why his garment evinces a combination of yellow and red, the colors of the House of Oldenburg. In light of the context, this feature can certainly be no coincidence, for it reflects the prince's origins.

Yet sovereignty of the Dukedom of Schleswig under Frederick III bore the seed of the tiny state's decline within itself. Without the aid of greater powers, above all Sweden, the Gottorf dukedom could not

*Jürgen Ovens, **Mother and Child in front of a Forest and Lake Landscape (Queen Hedwig Eleonora of Sweden and the Swedish Crown Prince Charles)**, late 1650s, oil on canvas, 35 x 31 ¼ in., Kulturstiftung des Landes Schleswig-Holstein*

assert itself in the face of Danish claims. When Sweden fell at the start of the eighteenth century, Gottorf went down with it.

After the Gottorf court was expelled by the Danish crown in the course of the eighteenth century, its movable properties gradually came to Copenhagen. Apart from the solidly installed and partly still surviving furnishings, very little remains of the period of the dukes of Schleswig-Holstein-Gottorf and Frederick III. In 1947, owing to the destruction of the old museum building in Kiel, the collections of the Schleswig-Holstein State Museums were moved from Kiel to Schleswig and Gottorf Palace, and the museum now began to concentrate on bringing together any still accessible pieces of Gottorf provenance. Its then director, Ernst Schlee (1910–1994), proceeded to lay the groundwork for the state collections in their present form.

JD

The Baroque Garden and the Gottorf Globe

Gottorf's fame as a flourishing residence and bastion of science and scholarship in the seventeenth century rested not only on the ducal *Kunstkammer* and its European renown, but also on the Baroque gar-

Ground plan of Palace Island and Neuwerk Garden *(from Laurids de Thurah,* Den Danske Vitruvius, *vol. II, 1749)*

den north of the palace, known as Neuwerk Garden. The elongated, five-level terraced park in the Italianate style and its special attraction at the center of the lowest terrace, an enterable terrestrial and celestial globe over 10 feet in diameter, were without precedence in northern Germany, or indeed anywhere in northern Europe.

These two unique Gottorf wonders are scheduled for reconstruction in the coming years, thanks to generous funding from the palace's Friends' Association.

Gottorf residents loved and devoted themselves to the art of gardening. After the West Garden and the Old Garden, which once extended south of the palace and have since sadly gone to ruin, the magnificent Neuwerk Garden was begun in 1637. Embedded in gently sloping, wooded terrain beyond the swampy low ground surrounding Palace Island and connected with it by a tree-lined causeway, the garden was laid out under the ambitious direction of Duke Frederick III and continued, after 1660, by his son, Duke Christian Albert. Though the garden has since run wild, its Baroque landscaping features are still recognizable, have never been altered or built on and can readily be reconstructed on the basis of numerous sources and documents.

Entering the garden over the causeway, visitors immediately come upon a small neoclassical temple with an elaborately decorated fountain and large octagonal basin. As if by way of welcome, the water god Triton sounds his horn. With this fanfare, the garden opens out on the left with the Königsallee, a historical avenue also known as Schleswig-Holstein-Allee. It invites a stroll beneath 150 shady lindens, replanted in the year 2000.

***Temple, cascade and fountain** of 1834 in Neuwerk Garden on the site of a submerged Baroque fountain*

Hercules Fighting the Hydra, 1997, replica of a Baroque sculpture (fragments of the original are in the stone sculpture collection, or Lapidarium, *of Gottorf Palace)*

On the opposite side is Hercules Pond. The idyllic rectangular pond, a favorite meeting place, is named after the mighty sculpture showing the mythological hero—the embodiment of royal virtue and power—in battle with the giant sea serpent, Hydra. Still much admired for its size alone, in the Baroque period this group was the largest free-standing sculpture in Schleswig-Holstein. Its broken fragments lay undiscovered in the pond until 1995, when they were recovered and the sculpture restored.

Once located behind the pond was Globe House, built to accommodate the imposing Giant Globe (see below). The series of terraces there decrease in size from bottom to top to create a perspective illusion. They were divided by symmetrically laid out paths, punctuated by fountains and water follies of various sizes and diversely planted geometrical beds, and framed by hedges and fruit trees. This magnificent garden must have afforded lovely walks. Promenaders enjoyed the view of ducal coats of arms and emblems formed of flowers, and statues of philosophers, mythological figures and allegories that were open to many interpretations.

The culmination of this interdisciplinary work of landscaping and visual art was undoubtedly the Giant Globe. Duke Frederick III ordered this masterpiece of artisanry, science and technology in 1650, from his court scholar, Adam Olearius. It was kept at the Globe

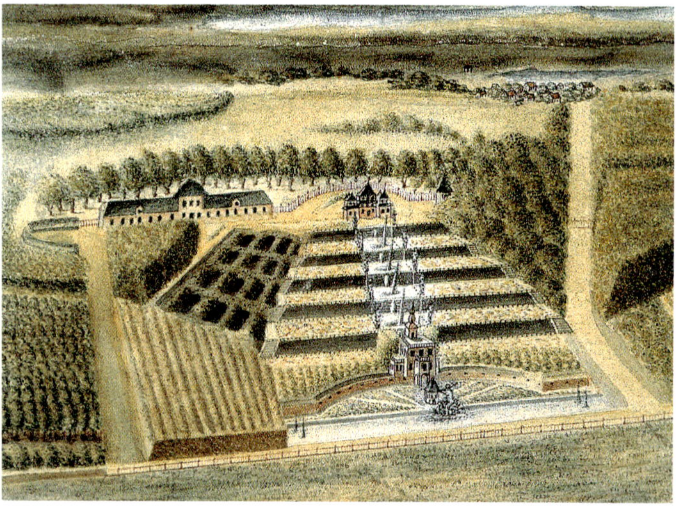

*Hans Christoffer Lönberg, **Bird's-eye View of Schleswig and Gottorf Palace, Neuwerk Garden** (detail), 1732, watercolor (Schleswig-Holsteinisches Landesarchiv, Sect. 402 BII, no. 247)*

House, also known as Friedrichsburg, erected at the top of a semicircular enclosure around Hercules Pond. Never before had a project of this type and scope been attempted. Over 10 feet in diameter, the surface of the globe bore a cartographically exact representation of the then known world and, inside, it had a wooden bench around its circumference that seated up to twelve people. The interior surface of the hollow sphere displayed the "entire" firmament, with elaborate figurative adornment, which illustrated the course of the planets and stars.

This amazing apparatus was set in motion by a water mill in the basement of Globe House. A transmission of finely adjusted worm gears and cogwheels, based on the latest clockmaking technology, made the globe revolve once around its axis every twenty-four hours. Anyone who found this too slow could use a hand crank to "move the world" themselves. One can well imagine that the terrestrial globe on the exterior and the unprecedented, candlelit "planetarium" in the interior, based on the Ptolemaic, geocentric view of the universe, must have struck visitors as a superb scientific and cosmological object that was incidentally also a marvelous and enjoyable carousel. This attraction, as it were the historical culmination of Baroque culture at Gottorf, brought the dukes of Schleswig high renown among European scholars.

Peter the Great's request that the globe be given to him in 1713, after Gottorf was defeated in the conflict with the Danish crown, is sufficient indication of its fame and significance. The czar, who took a keen interest in science, had the globe removed from Friedrichsburg

Felix Lühning, ***The Giant Globe in the Globe House,*** *1997, reconstruction*

and transported to St. Petersburg, which had been founded shortly before. Even more than the removal of the treasury and library to Copenhagen in 1749, or the loss of the other scientific apparatus, the loss of the Giant Globe came to be synonymous with the end of Gottorf's heyday.

After the empty Globe House was demolished in 1768, the garden began to decay. In the eighteenth and nineteenth centuries the other garden buildings were razed, including Amalienburg, a large pleasure seat at the top of the uppermost terrace. Finally Gottorf

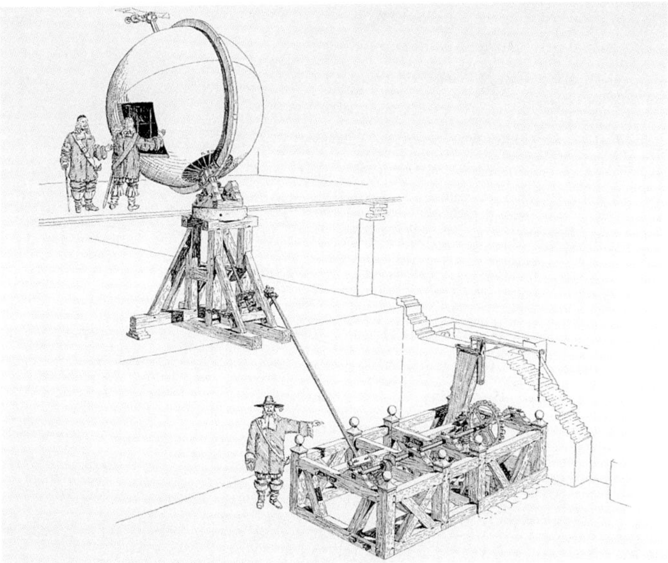

Felix Lühning, ***Drive for Operating the Globe,*** *1997, reconstruction*

Palace became first a Danish, then a Prussian, barracks, and the graded terraces served as drill fields for cavalry and infantry. It was not until 1948 that the vegetation and woods now in evidence were planted.

The ambitious project of the State Museum Foundation (Stiftung Schleswig-Holsteinische Landesmuseen Schloss Gottorf) to reconstruct the Giant Globe, a building to house it and the garden itself is drawing closer to realization. It will signal the recovery of a unique ensemble of art and landscape design of great historical and cultural value, especially as regards the history of Schleswig-Holstein. The garden design will be based on details of the historical planting and flora, and will include cuts and vistas that convey an impression of the original landscaping. Yet the globe and the idyllic microcosm of the garden will represent much more than a relic of Baroque ostentation or a testament to an early scientific achievement. The terrestrial and celestial globe, which at its time stood for an inviolable conception of the universe, illustrates as under a magnifying glass the long intellectual path from a mechanical, anthropocentric view of the world, through the consequences of the Copernican revolution, down to our present, much less consistent and self-confident world-view.

TP

Five Centuries of Furniture: From Medieval Cupboard to Art Nouveau Interior

Furniture holds a special place in our decorative arts collection, in terms of both quality and quantity. Exceptionally well represented is northern German furniture from the late medieval to the Baroque period. These pieces are characterized, on the one hand, by richly carved decor and, on the other, by a certain conservatism. Medieval furniture types, such as chests and *Schenkschieven*, cupboards for precious tableware, enjoyed a very long tradition in this area.

Cupboard *(*Schenkschieve*), early 16th century (frames and cornice date from 1656), Pellworm, Husum (?), oak, painted (fluting panels in tempera; frames on the front and sides in oil), 84 ⅝ x 69 ¼ x 26 ⅜ in.*

A good example is our cupboard from Pellworm, made of oak and magnificently painted. The panels on the front and doors date from the early sixteenth century. They evince skillfully carved fluting-panel motifs, a typical late-Gothic form of ornament developed from the technique of planing. The frames and historical revival cornice, on the other hand, stem from a later period. The color scheme is likewise varied in age. While the fluting-panel fields still bear the original blue and red tempera finish, the frames on the front and the side fields are decorated with figurative depictions in oil, for instance of David and Goliath. An inscription gives the date and client of the later work: in 1656 Catharina Ockens evidently had the cupboard refurbished in memory of her deceased husband, Ocke Harrsen of Pellworm.

Although the piece was "modernized" and made over into a kind of memorial to the owner's family, retention of its basic medieval structure shows a respect for tradition. Cupboards of this type were typical features of northern German furnishing from the fifteenth to the seventeenth century, and they were often required pieces, assigned by furnituremakers' guilds, to attain the title of master. *Schenkschieven* (literally, serving panels or boards) were cupboards with several doors, and were usually permanently installed, that is, built into the wainscot or wall paneling. The middle door, or *Schieve*, was originally hinged at the bottom, to open downward. In an open position, it was used to display valuable tableware, and to serve beverages. The flap-door of the present piece was apparently converted into a normally hinged door at some later date.

Susanna Cupboard, ca. 1580, oak with intarsia strips in walnut, lindenwood and ebony, 81 7/8 x 48 7/8 x 24 3/8 in.

A further example of this type of furniture is a piece known as the "Susanna Cupboard" of about 1580. One of the oldest and most important additions to the collection, it can be traced back to a personal purchase on the part of Gustav Thaulow, professor at Kiel University. Thaulow's collection of northern German medieval and Renaissance woodcarvings formed the nucleus of today's State Museum of Art and Cultural History.

In terms of structure, the piece is based on the cupboard type described above. The middle door was originally designed as a flap and, as in the Pellworm cupboard, was later converted into a side-hinged door. The figurative depictions have a religious content. The relief carving illustrates the story of Susanna and the Elders. Other figures include Adam and Eve, and personifications of the cardinal virtues of Faith and Hope. The figure in the central niche is lost, but it certainly represented a personification of Love, or Charity. The figures are conceived as architectural elements known as herm pilasters. This motif, like the lower, indented fields with putti, reflect an orientation to Netherlandish patterns. Artists such as Cornelis Floris, in whose Antwerp shop the funerary memorial to Frederick I in Schleswig Cathedral was created, contributed materially to the spread of the Renaissance style in northern Germany.

Although nothing is known about the designer of the Susanna Cupboard, its harmonious overall proportions, the balance between carved decor and construction, and the lucid division of its sections make it a masterpiece of northern German Renaissance furniture-making.

Like cupboards, carved chests were popular pieces of furniture in the region's prosperous households. The best-known cabinetmakers in this field included Hans Gudewerdt the Elder, of Eckernförde, and Heinrich Ringerinck, of Flensburg. Pieces from both of their workshops have been in our collection ever since the days of the Thaulow Museum in Kiel.

The front panels of Gudewerdt's "Small Esther Chest" bear scenes from the eponymous Old Testament story. The depictions are captioned with inscriptions in Low German in the socle area. The

*Hans Gudewerdt the Elder (ca. 1570–ca. 1642), **Small Esther Chest**, 1609, oak (new lid), 22 ⅞ x 59 ⅞ x 24 ⅜ in.*

middle pilaster strip beneath the warrior figure bears the date 1609. Esther, the young Israelite girl who saved her people by charming the Persian King Ahasuerus with her beauty and courage, was frequently depicted on carved chests of the era. As a biblical love story with a moral, it was well suited to the function of such elaborate pieces, which in well-to-do families were often part of the bride's trousseau.

Although the three-dimensional treatment of figures and ornament suggests an affinity with the Baroque, such chests were basically a conservative type of furniture. Northern German clients and artisans maintained traditional furniture forms down to the seventeenth century and beyond, until richer families gradually began to replace their chests and cupboards with imposing, commodious cabinets known as *Schapps.* Yet even here, traditional carving in solid wood held its own against the introduction of the modern veneer technique.

Carvers and cabinetmakers displayed their skills not only in the field of furniture but in that of paneling as well. One of the most significant northern German paneled rooms, from the original furnishings of Gottorf Palace, has survived, and brooks comparison with late Renaissance furniture. Made from 1610 to 1615 by court cabinetmaker Andreas Salgen and woodcarver Jürgen Gower, it was built

Cabinet illustrated opposite, in closed position

*Conrad Geisler, **cabinet**, ca. 1710–20, Altona, carcass: oak, pine, cedar, mahogany, veneer: mahogany, ebony and other exotic woods, ivory, bone, mother of pearl, metal mounts: polished steel with gold inlay, 59 7/8 x 38 5/8 x 16 3/4 in., Kulturstiftung der Länder, der Beauftragte der Bundesregierung für Angelegenheiten der Kultur und der Medien, Kulturstiftung des Landes Schleswig-Holstein, Freundeskreis Schloss Gottorf e.V. and Arthur Boskamp, Hamburg*

into the chapel as the Duke of Schleswig's private oratory (see pp. 106, 126). In this case, the carvings are supplemented by rich intarsia work.

The intarsia technique involves carving ornamental shapes out of variously colored types of wood and setting them into the wood of the piece, which remains visible. In marquetry, in contrast, thin pieces of wood, ivory or mother of pearl veneer are composed into pictures and glued over structural components of inferior wood, thus concealing them. A fine example of this technique is seen in our cabinet with *chinoiserie* decor, acquired in 1998. Belonging to the category of aristocratic Baroque furnishings, the piece was made about 1710–20, for an as yet unidentified client. The ascription was made on the basis of similar elaborate furniture at Rosenborg Royal Palace in Copenhagen, which, according to the inventory there, was crafted by a cabinetmaker from Altona by the name of Conrad Geisler. Cabinets of this type were favorite status symbols from the sixteenth century onward. Apart from serving purposes of display, they were also used to store collections.

The depictions on the piece are invaluable in terms of cultural history. They were based on illustrations in *China illustrata*, a book by the Jesuit priest Athanasius Kircher (1602–1680), published in Amsterdam in 1667, in which the successes of Roman-Catholic missionaries in China were recorded. The use of detailed depictions of foreign customs as furniture decor can be explained by the enthusiasm that obtained at that period for Near and Far Eastern art and culture. In this connection, mention should be made of the Oriental expedition mounted by the Gottorf court. As early as the 1630s, Duke Frederick III sent an expedition to Persia, whose yield was documented in Adam Olearius's *Moskowitische und Persianische Reisebeschreibung* (Description of Muscovite and Persian Travels), first published in 1647 in Schleswig (the second, revised edition was reprinted frequently).

Chinese designs in the marquetry technique are also a feature of the secretary by Anton Gottfried Lindemann, dating from about 1760. Yet here the decor, freer and more imaginative in design, anticipates the Rococo style. Secretaries with a fold-down writing surface and set on a chest of drawers became a very popular type of furniture in northern Germany in the eighteenth century. In analogy to the Danish term for secretary, *chatol*, such pieces were also called *Aufsatzschatullen* in Schleswig-Holstein. As status symbols they replaced their predecessors of similar type, the tall cabinets of the Renaissance and Baroque periods.

The skilled employment of thin veneers, whether to cover large surfaces or for figurative or ornamental marquetry decor, was among the main tasks of eighteenth-century cabinetmakers, who were also known as *ébènistes* (after the French word for ebony). Lindemann, active in Kiel, was one of the major practitioners of this craft in northern Germany. His oeuvre is represented by several specimens in the State Museum collection. Lindemann enjoyed a reputation far beyond the borders of Kiel, his clientele including aristocratic and well-to-do middle-class families from all over Schleswig-Holstein.

Characteristic of Lindemann are virtuoso floral marquetries, seen here on the cabinet doors, combined with highly idiosyncratic figurative designs in the Chinese style. The plain, straightforward, basic form of the piece clearly reveals the influence of English furniture. The rigor of its contours is mitigated by the slightly concave drawer fronts and the curving top, in which echoes of Rococo are evident.

Not even Art Nouveau furniture designers, who strove for an unprecedented, modern style, could do entirely without historical patterns. The Schleswig furniture collection, which contains pieces dating from the Middle Ages to the present day, provides a wonderful opportunity to study such links at first hand.

Anton Gottfried Lindemann (1706–1787), ***secretary****, ca. 1760, Kiel, carcass: oak, part coniferous woods, veneer: walnut, maple, ash curlwood and other native woods, brass, 92 ½ x 46 ⅛ x 24 in., Kulturstiftung des Landes Schleswig-Holstein*

A good case in point is the bedroom designed in 1905 by Hans Christiansen, an artist and artisan of Flensburg, for Anna Markowitz, the German-Jewish proprietor of a furniture store in Sibiu, Transylvania. A typical feature of Christiansen's creations is their subtle display of color. In this case, visual accents are provided by red-tinted oval fields on the upper sections of the bedroom furniture. These are framed by neoclassical wreath and leaf ornaments. Like many of his contemporaries, Christiansen oscillated between modern and historically oriented design principles. While his designs were straightforward and functional, they were nevertheless based on traditional models in which Christiansen found just these qualities. He took inspiration both from late medieval furniture and the folk, peasant furniture of his Schleswig-Holstein homeland, yet without ever slavishly copying their style.

Christiansen, who spent several years in Paris and joined the famous Darmstadt artists' colony in 1899, was among the major artists of the Art Nouveau period (see pp. 71–76). More of his works —paintings and drawings as well as crafts pieces—are on display at Gottorf. That so typical striving of the period to create *Gesamtkunstwerke* (total works of art) is especially evident in Christiansen's case. He was simultaneously a painter and an interior designer, and did not think in terms of conventional artistic hierarchies. His bedroom suite indicatively contains painterly elements, such as the intarsia on the occasional table. In a manner recalling Symbolist painting, it represents a woman in profile with stylized strands of hair and floral ornament. *CK*

Eighteenth-Century Treasures: The Baltic Faience Collection

Faiences from the Baltic Sea region are on display at Gottorf in great richness and variety. These ceramics, glazed a creamy white and delicately painted, were popular throughout Europe in the eighteenth century. Those who could not afford china, which was still very costly and reserved for the nobility, purchased faience, with its tin-based glaze and porcelain-like decor, for their tables and living rooms. Factories existed in Holland and France, Germany and Switzerland. Others were soon established throughout the Baltic trade region, in the area of present-day Schleswig-Holstein, Denmark, Sweden, Norway and the Baltic countries.

Especially interesting are the personal connections that grew up among the manufactories, beyond all language barriers. Germans, Scandinavians and some Frenchmen worked side by side in faience

*Store Kongensgade manufactory, Copenhagen, **"bishop" punchbowl**, faience, cobalt blue in high-temperature color, Johann Ernst Pfau period (1727–49), painted decoration: Johann Heinrich Pfau, h. 12 5/8 in., diam. 9 3/4 in., Axel Springer Collection*

manufacturing, and migrated from one enterprise to another when their expertise was in demand.

The Store Kongensgade faience manufactory in Copenhagen is the oldest of its kind in the Baltic region. It was founded in 1722, and continued to operate until 1779. During the company's first two years, Johann Wolff, a native of Holstein, served as chief foreman. Then Wolff transferred to the Swedish factory of Rörstrand. His position in Copenhagen was filled for the next two decades by Johann Ernst Pfau, a German ceramicist, who was followed in 1749 by a Dane, Christian Girløf.

Punchbowls known as "bishops," like the one from Copenhagen illustrated here, were a specialty of northern European faience production. Most of the surviving examples stem from Store Kongensgade, yet imitations were manufactured at many other sites around the Baltic Sea, including Schleswig, Kiel, Rendsburg, Kellinghusen and Stralsund in Germany, and Herrebøe in Norway.

Bishops used to serve a punch of the same name which was popular all around northern Europe, and consisted of red wine, bitter orange or lemon juice and sugar. The peculiar drinking customs associated with this beverage can presumably be traced back to Protestant resentments against Catholics. In eighteenth-century Copenhagen, a group known as the Pope Society regularly convened at inns and held satirical skits in which its members played various roles in the Catholic church hierarchy. A link between this merry association and the emergence of special punchbowls would seem likely, especially as there is another variant of the drink called "cardinal," made of white wine and orange juice.

Kiel manufactory, ***potpourri vase****, faience, various muffle colors, Johann Georg Bonifaz Buchwald period (1768–71), painted decoration: Abraham Leihamer, h. 12 5/8 in., diam. 7 7/8 in.*

Characteristic of Copenhagen faiences is their blue and white decor, which, by way of Dutch patterns, ultimately stemmed from the tradition of Chinese porcelain. In the extended Danish state, which in that period included Schleswig, Store Kongensgade held a monopoly on decor in cobalt blue. This led a Schleswig manufactory, which was founded in 1755, to specialize in manganese purple, as seen, for instance, in a tureen and two candlesticks displayed here.

The finest Schleswig-Holstein faiences came from the manufactory in Kiel. Its specialties included potpourris—jars designed to contain an aromatic mixture of flower petals, herbs, spices, fragrances and salt. Previously, such mixtures had been gathered and stored throughout the year in clay pots, which were thus rendered unusable for any other purpose. These pots were referred to as "pots pourris" (rotten pots), a term subsequently transferred to their decorative counterparts. Potpourris were placed on stoves or in stove niches during the wintertime. Their decor was frequently based on engravings by the Augsburg artist Johann Esaias Nilson, like the *commedia dell'arte* scene illustrated here.

The Kiel faience company was headed from 1763 by Johann Samuel Friedrich Tännich, who had previously worked in Meissen, Strasbourg and Frankenthal. Many Kiel pieces reflect the influence of porcelain and French faience, especially as regards their floral decor,

Kiel manufactory, ***table service****, including a centerpiece, small tureen, plates and platters, faience, various muffle colors, painted decoration of centerpiece: Johann Leihamer, Johann Georg Bonifaz Buchwald period (1768–71), painted decoration of tureen: Johann Andreas Riehl, Johann Samuel Friedrich Tännich period (1763–68), centerpiece: h. 16 ½ in., tureen: h. 16 ½ in., diam. 13 ¾ x 8 ¾ in.*

for which Tännich recruited specialists from Strasbourg. On view in the Rococo Department are several laid tables, including one with beautiful examples of this floral decor. They convey an idea of the effect of fine faiences in the setting of an eighteenth-century interior. The white and gold wall paneling in the adjacent room, from Plön Palace, provides an authentic ambience.

A fascinating dialogue with the Schleswig-Holstein faiences is introduced by those from Scandinavia and Revel (present-day Tallinn, Estonia), which originate almost exclusively from the Springer Collection. While the earliest acquisitions of Schleswig-Holstein faiences go back to the days of the Thaulow Museum in Kiel, the collection of the publisher Axel Springer came to the museum in 1997, thanks to a generous donation on the part of his wife, Friede Springer, and his heirs. It represented a significant enrichment, and in many instances a welcome supplement, to the existing faience collection.

A marvelous example of Scandinavian faience is seen in our centerpiece from Rörstrand in Sweden. Adorned with the figures of Triton blowing his horn and a Nereid, it represents a small-scale version of a motif popular in fountain sculpture of the day.

The exchange of personnel among factories in the Baltic region is exemplified above all by Johann Georg Bonifaz Buchwald. Before becoming Tännich's successor in Kiel, Buchwald was active, among other places, at Marieberg in Sweden and in Eckernförde. After his Kiel period, he went on to Stockelsdorf. Every time he moved, Buchwald took his best assistants with him. This resulted in the close aes-

Rörstrand manufactory, Sweden, ***centerpiece and matching platter****, 1762, faience, manganese purple in high-temperature colors, Elias Magnus Ingman-Nordenstolpe period (1753–73), painted decoration: Carl Erik Löfström, centerpiece: 9 1/4 x 12 1/4 x 7 1/2 in., platter: 1 3/8 x 19 1/2 x 12 1/4 in., Axel Springer Collection*

Marieberg manufactory, Sweden, ***top of a tea table****, faience; red, green, blue, brown and yellow muffle colors, Pierre Berthevin period (1766–69) or Henrik Sten period (1769–88), painted decoration: probably Franz Henrik Frantzen, l. 35 1/4 in., w. 23 5/8 in., Axel Springer Collection*

thetic affinities often found among the pieces from the companies just mentioned.

Marieberg was the source of our lovely tea-table top with its depiction of a Swedish sailing ship and a fantastic seascape. In the eighteenth century, hot beverages such as tea, coffee and cocoa, enjoyed increasing popularity in high social circles. Tea tables developed from functional pieces of furniture into works of art in their own right, which perfectly harmonized with the pastel color schemes of Rococo interiors. Owing to the large size of their faience top, tea tables of this kind were especially difficult to manufacture. The Schleswig collection contains a total of forty-one such pieces from factories in the Baltic area, including eleven Schleswig-Holstein examples from the original museum stocks. The remainder stem from the Axel Springer Collection.

Overall view of tea table illustrated above

Toward the end of the eighteenth century, cheaper stoneware increasingly supplanted faience, and nearly all the northern European factories went out of business. Those in Kellinghusen managed to adapt to the changing market in another way. Around the turn of the century they shifted their focus from the elaborately decorated faiences of previous years to more popular, "mass-produced" goods (see pp. 177–81). Material and technique remained the same, but the decor was simplified and made more schematic. The brightly colored Kellinghusen faiences were intended for new buyers in rural farming areas, especially the marshlands. Thanks to their new line, the Kellinghusen factories were able to survive until the middle of the nineteenth century. An example of their early production is a piece known as the "maternity tureen," which was surely intended as a gift to a young mother in memory of the birth of her child. *CK*

"Yearn for the education, art, wisdom and honor of men": Portraits at Gottorf Palace of and by Women of the 18th and 19th Centuries

Although women were frequently portrayed in eighteenth- and nineteenth-century art, portraits by women artists were the exception.

Gottorf's full-length portrait of Caroline Amalie of Denmark was done in 1845 by the Danish painter Johan Vilhelm Gertner. The Danish queen is clad in a purple velvet dress whose sheen is offset by

Johan Vilhelm Gertner (1818–1871), ***Queen Caroline Amalie of Denmark,*** *1845, oil on canvas, 90 3/4 x 61 5/8 in.*

Anna Rosina Matthieu (née Lisiewska) (1713–1783), ***Johanna Elizabeth, Princess of Holstein-Gottorf, Princess of Anhalt-Zerbst*** *(1712–1760), ca. 1752, oil on canvas, 56 1/4 x 43 1/4 in.*

white lace and satin trim. She stands on one of those large carpets designed for unusually large rooms, above her a heavy green velvet curtain, behind her a damast wall-covering with broad red stripes. This is the interior of her study at Sorgenfri Palace outside Copenhagen. We look in vain for insignia of power, such as the Russian Order of St. Catherine, the Gottorf Order of St. Anne or even a royal ermine. Such insignia are found in a portrait of Johanna Elizabeth, Princess of Holstein-Gottorf and Princess of Anhalt-Zerbst, executed about 1752 by Anna Rosina Matthieu (1713–1783). The artist, whose maiden name was Lisiewska, was a sister of the painter Anna Dorothea Therbusch.

The only traditional, noble attribute in Gertner's painting is the curtain, a motif that had already begun to appear in bourgeois portraits by that time. But what really distinguishes Caroline Amalie as a royal personage is her great writing desk. Middle-class women in the Biedermeier and following period, from which the queen's portrait dates, were predestined for a life as spouse, mother and housewife. Unlike the respected elderly woman author Sophie von La Roche, they would probably have ruined their chances of marrying, or even their reputation, by having themselves depicted with this piece of furniture, which had no place in their daily routine or career. Yet, even La Roche, whose portrait at her desk in front of a well-stocked bookcase was perhaps the earliest of its type in Germany, admitted in a brochure titled "My Desk," " … as soon as someone comes, my handiwork appears, which I love as much as my papers and books; especially since I have noticed that men of high birth and intellect show me even more respect for the domestic industry of my needle than for the occupation of my pen." This was written in 1799, when more self-determination for women at least seemed possible. As

*Angelika Kauffmann (1741–1807), **Julia von Reventlow**, 1784, oil on canvas, 50 3/8 x 40 1/2 in.*

queen, Caroline Amalie, who enjoyed an intellectual partnership with her husband, could take a desk for granted some fifty years later.

Somewhat earlier than Sophie von La Roche's brochure, in the latter half of the eighteenth century, hopeful beginnings had been made. People mingled in literary salons, irrespective of social standing or gender. The ideal of friendship found expression in "friendship temples"—and in paintings such as that of Julia von Reventlow, daughter of the banker and prime minister of Frederick II of Denmark, Heinrich Carl Schimmelmann. Friedrich von Reventlow commissioned this portrait of his wife from Angelika Kauffmann (1741–1807) during a stay in Rome in December 1783. He described the result in January 1784: "She is depicted at the moment of buoyantly welcoming a friend, brother or sister with open arms. The expression is fine and good, and the pose as gracious as can be expected of the woman painter." Julia von Reventlow's gown recalls the work of Kauffmann's French fellow-artist Elisabeth Vigée-Lebrun, who always kept a considerable number of shawls in her studio in order to clad her sitters in the "Greek fashion," and who likewise preferred them to pose without wigs. And the picture bears stylistic affinities with the portraits of Sir Joshua Reynolds, with whom Kauffmann was often, and disparagingly, compared.

In this portrait painted in Rome, Kauffmann captures Julia von Reventlow's outgoing character, that of a woman who not only kept open house for a large circle of friends and intellectuals, but also worked to abolish slavery and wrote books to educate the rural populace. Thus she played the role of the high-born lady, endeavoring to live her life in conformance with credos such as those advanced by the Schlegel brothers and Novalis in their "Catechism of Reason for Noble Women." Published in 1798 as one of the fragments in their journal, *Athenäum*, it reads, "I believe in infinite humanity, which was in existence before it assumed the cloak of masculinity and femininity. I believe that I live not to obey or to amuse myself, but to be and become; and I believe in the power of will and education to help me once again approach the infinite, to release me from the fetters of ignorance and to make me independent of the constrictions of sex."

Johann Heinrich Wilhelm Tischbein the Younger (1751–1829) served as director of the Naples Academy until 1799, when he fled from advancing Napoleonic troops and returned to Germany. Tischbein sought out August Wilhelm Schlegel, who was professor in Jena. During a stay in Göttingen, the artist, also known as the "Eutiner" or "Goethe Tischbein," established a "drawing course for ladies." About 1812—or later—Tischbein painted a portrait of his wife and their five daughters. In view of their date of marriage, 1806, and the age of the eldest daughter portrayed, the work was probably not executed until about 1820. It shows a clear stylistic affinity with the work of Philipp Otto Runge, yet the simplicity and straightforward-

Johann Heinrich Wilhelm Tischbein the Younger (1751–1829), ***The Artist's Wife and Five Daughters at Breakfast****, ca. 1812, oil on canvas, 49 ¼ x 39 in., Kulturstiftung des Landes Schleswig-Holstein*

ness of Tischbein's well-nigh monochrome rendering were entirely original at the time. He was concerned with the effects of light, its reflections in the vessels, the motif of the hand with candlelight shining through and the informal gathering of his family. One is again reminded of the "Catechism" of the Schlegel brothers and Novalis, whose fifth commandment reads: "Honor the uniqueness and caprice of your children, so that they may be happy and live vigorously on earth."

A short time later, in 1821, Louise Seidler (1786–1866) painted the portrait *Friederike Juliane, Countess Baudissin, with a View of Florence.* While spending most of the period from 1818 to 1823 in Rome, in 1820–21 the artist enjoyed "the quiet and a regular life" in Florence. She copied Raphael Madonnas and a Perugino Archangel Michael, entirely in keeping with the art of the Nazarenes, with whom she had become associated in Rome. Although the Brotherhood of St. Luke admitted no female members, this did not affect Seidler's friendly feelings toward them.

During her stay in Florence, the Baudissin family took Seidler under their wing. Their aid included the commission of this portrait of the music-loving countess, clad in a Renaissance-style costume and playing a harp, against the background of a Florentine scene in

Louise Seidler (1786–1866), ***Friederike Juliane, Countess Baudissin, with a View of Florence****, 1821, oil on canvas, 72 7/8 x 44 1/4 in.*

which the Arno River and the Palazzo Vecchio can be seen in front of a hazy, distant landscape. The depiction of the young Friederike Juliane listening to the fading notes as her fingers glide over the strings reflects Seidler's involvement with Raphael and Perugino, but also her affinity with the Nazarenes, such as Julius Schnorr von Carolsfeld and his portrait of Clara Bianca von Quandt.

Louise Seidler belonged to a generation of women artists who, unlike the Lisiewska sisters or Elisabeth Vigée-Lebrun in the eighteenth century, were no longer trained in their fathers' workshops but overcame many obstacles to go their own way. She was encouraged to develop her drawing talent by an aunt with whom she lived for a time and who put her through boarding school. After graduation, however, Seidler had to earn money for additional—and secret—drawing lessons by working as a seamstress, which she despised. Yet what this and the preceding generation of female artists did have in common was their dependence on support from noble families who were ready to believe in "infinite humanity."

These few examples represent only a tiny part of the rich painting collection at Gottorf Palace. On the one hand, its composition reflects the history of the dukes of Schleswig-Holstein-Gottorf, to whom the collection owes not only its portraits but its works by Lucas Cranach. At least twelve Cranachs, now in Copenhagen, came to Gottorf in 1630 as the dowry of Maria Elizabeth of Saxony when she wed Frederick III. Another thrust of the museum's collecting activity derives from the dukes' enthusiasm for Netherlandish art, which made up a large part of their collection. Finally, during the Danish period of south Schleswig in the eighteenth and nineteenth centuries, the art of the Golden Age in Denmark, which emerged from the Copenhagen Academy, exerted a strong influence on northern German painting. *MS*

Socrates Walking on Air: The Department of Prints and Drawings

Socrates in a Basket, a pen-and-ink drawing by Asmus Jakob Carstens (1754–1798), was probably done in Berlin in 1791, the year of Mozart's death. Born in St. Jürgen, near Schleswig, Carstens was

Asmus Jakob Carstens (1754–1798), ***Socrates in a Basket****, 1791, pen and ink, 11 1/8 x 7 in.*

apprenticed against his will to a wine dealer of Eckernförde. He taught himself to draw and paint, to such good effect that he was accepted into the Copenhagen Academy. After 1790 he was a professor at the Berlin Academy of Arts and Mechanical Sciences, before leaving this post to spend his final years, from 1792 until his death, as an independent artist in Rome.

Although the composition shows affinities with the stringent spirit of the *opera seria*, recalling Mozart's last opera, *La Clemenza di Tito*, of the same year, it is not without a humorous note. The treatment of the figures is oriented to Michelangelo and Raphael, whose Vatican frescoes Carstens had already seen in reproductions before his yearning to visit the Eternal City was fulfilled. His first Italian journey, undertaken from Copenhagen with friends in 1783, had got no farther than Milan and Mantua owing to lack of funds. At any rate, Carstens was able to study the frescoes of Giulio Romano, from the immediate orbit of Raphael, at the Palazzo del Tè there.

In his comedy *The Clouds*, here illustrated by Carstens, Aristophanes attacks the immoral argumentation of the Sophists, who are represented, of all people, by Socrates. The indebted peasant Strepsiades hopes to learn from him how to shake off his creditors with clever rhetoric. In the drawing, the philosopher's pupils are represented like the biblical prophets in the Sistine Chapel at the Vatican, darkly threatening or earnestly collected. This characterization would have drawn justified criticism from Goethe, because it seems to anticipate the oppressive inactivity of the Romantic spirit that he attacked so harshly. Still, these already quite elderly pupils form merely a backdrop for the lively, reverberating dispute between Strepsiades and their mentor.

In the figure of the peasant, Carstens portrayed his Berlin friend, the architect Johann Christian Genelli, with whom he collaborated and who perhaps suggested the subject to him. In contrast to this "ennobled" peasant, the figure of Socrates appears in a humble rush basket, hovering above the scene like a *deus ex machina*. The unity achieved between the grotesque nature of this idea and the dignity of the other figures is much to the artist's credit. Nineteenth-century history painting lacks precisely this balance, which Goethe described as a unity of seriousness and play. In its development from Jacques-Louis David and Jean-Auguste-Dominique Ingres to Karl von Piloty and Hans Makart, this venerable genre time and again crossed the borderline into the ridiculous, which led to its crisis and eventually its demise.

The Gottorf drawing originates from the collection of Count Friedrich and Countess Julia von Reventlow, who acquired it from the artist in Rome in 1796. A less successful version in sepia from Carstens's estate was honored by a reproduction in Goethe's publication of the Weimar Collection in 1821. Under the title of "Socrates

Walking on Air," the drawing was aptly described as "… a parody in the high style … a satire without caricature; it is a perfect expression of [Carstens's] art and thinking in this genre. Aristophanes' *Clouds* provided the occasion for the picture. This wag, wishing to get the better of a natural philosopher in the mask of Socrates rising above the community and to make the crowd look ridiculous, has him appear in a stage-machinery basket, suspended in the air and contemplating the sun. The poses of his students are quite strangely presented to a rural fellow coming on the scene, who wishes to have Socrates instruct his son, and we are given an indirect description of this auditorium. The art lover pleasurably perceives Carstens's angle on the text by proxy, when he finds himself immediately placed in the role of Strepsiades."

Taking this drawing as a point of departure to review the Gottorf Department of Prints and Drawings, let us now turn to works by Johann Heinrich Wilhelm Tischbein and Caspar David Friedrich's portrait drawing of Christian Friedrich Rühs, a historian from Greifswald. Going back further into the past, there are Netherlandish

Horst Janssen (1929–1995), ***poster design for Gottorf Palace****, 1986, color pencil, 29 1/8 x 18 7/8 in.*

Friedrich Karl Gotsch (1900–1984), ***Evening Landscape,*** *1938, pastels, 18 1/8 x 26 5/8 in.*

drawings from the seventeenth century and prints from the sixteenth, outstanding among which are works by Melchior Lorck of Flensburg.

Dating from the beginnings of the Gottorf collection at the Thaulow Museum in Kiel are extensive stocks of ornamental engravings, primarily from the seventeenth century. These were brought together by museum director Ernst Sauermann, who was beholden to the idea of a pattern collection for artisans of the kind promulgated by the nineteenth-century Arts and Crafts Movement. Also amassed at this period were the remarkable portrait collection and the topographical collection, focusing on Schleswig-Holstein. After the museum moved into Gottorf Palace following the war, it acquired the estates of Johann Holtz, a Flensburg calligrapher, and Hans Olde, artist and director of the Weimar Academy. The holdings of prints and drawings by Schleswig-Holstein and Hamburg artists were expanded, with certain key emphases. Gottorf now possesses a number of complete graphic oeuvres, including those of Friedel Anderson, Edgar Augustin, Gisela Bührmann, Charles Crodel, Harald Duwe, Klaus Fussmann, Jörn Pfab, Hans Sperschneider and Georg Tappert, in addition to large groups of works by such classical modern artists as Erich Heckel, Oskar Kokoschka and Christian Rohlfs (including a number of the latter's printing plates).

Gottorf also boasts 750 works by Horst Janssen (1929–1995), one of the largest collections of this artist's work anywhere. This we owe largely to the generosity of Janssen himself, who declared Gottorf

HAP Grieshaber (1909–1981), ***The Story of Joseph: His Brothers Falling on Their Knees before Him****, 1970, pastel chalks, ink and pencil on paper, 46 ⅛ x 56 ¼ in.*

to be his "mausoleum on paper" and for some years regularly donated impressions of his latest prints. Like most of the extensive oeuvre collections, these works are published in a stock catalogue, as well as those of Ernst Barlach, Gottfried Brockmann, Friedrich Karl Gotsch, HAP Grieshaber, Richard Haizmann, Diether Kressel, Volker Meier and Paul Wunderlich. Less thoroughly represented but present in superb examples are Eduard Bargheer, Willi Baumeister, Conrad Felixmüller, Ernst Ludwig Kirchner, Wolfgang Klähn, Edvard Munch, Rolf Nesch, Emil Nolde, Max Pechstein, Bernard Schultze, Emil Schumacher, Max Uhlig and Gustav Heinrich Wolff.

The photographic collection, apart from considerable earlier stocks, is distinguished by the Fritz Kempe Collection and fine groups of works by Ulrich Mack, Albert Renger-Patzsch and Karin Székessy.

TG

Life as a *Gesamtkunstwerk*: The Art Nouveau Department

A dinner plate, a soup plate, a small carafe, a liqueur glass, a knife, fork and spoon—these objects in the Gottorf collection bear witness to a major Art Nouveau *Gesamtkunstwerk*, or total work of art, Hans Christiansen's house "In Rosen" on Mathildenhöhe in Darmstadt. Sadly, it was the only building in the extraordinary Jugendstil complex that was destroyed in World War II and not reconstructed.

During preparations for the 1900 World Fair in Paris, several professors who had been called to the Darmstadt artists' colony the previous year (Hans Christiansen, Ludwig Habich, Josef Maria Olbrich, Rudolf Bosselt, Paul Bürck, Peter Behrens and Patriz Huber) decided on a project. On the hill known as Mathildenhöhe overlooking the town, artists' houses in the new style, Art Nouveau (called "Jugendstil" in the German-speaking world), would be erected. In accordance with the tenets of the Arts and Crafts Movement, each building would be a *Gesamtkunstwerk* down to the last detail, dedicated to a national revival of the crafts and good taste. The results would be presented at an exhibition in 1901.

All the houses, apart from that by the architect Peter Behrens, were designed by Josef Maria Olbrich, based in part on the ideas of individual artists involved, who also created the interior designs. Hans Christiansen (1866–1945) chose the rose as the motif of his house. Various rose designs adorned carpets, wallpaper and curtains, lamps, stained-glass windows and furniture, even the dress and lace collar worn by the lady of the house. Later known as the Christiansen rose, this motif, framed by parallel lines, served as the key element of a gold decor on delicate porcelain and simple, elegant glassware, and the lines became the basic motif on the silverware.

Hans Christiansen, Krautheim and Adelberg, Selb, ***plate from table service,*** *ca. 1903, porcelain, diam. 9 7/8 in.*

These tableware designs, which fulfilled the demand of truth to materials, were finished in time for the exhibition. The china and glassware were probably not manufactured until 1903, by Krautheim and Adelberg in Selb and the crystal manufactory in Theresienthal, respectively, whereas the silverware was produced by

Hans Christiansen, Theresienthal crystal manufactory, ***liqueur glass and carafe,*** *with rose motif, ca. 1903, glass, glass: h. 5 ⅛ in., carafe: h. 9 ⅞ in.*

Bruckmann and Sons in Heilbronn about 1901. However, in 1902 Christiansen had already withdrawn from the artists' colony, on account of budget cuts and "bureaucratic control." In the summer he continued to live at "In Rosen," but spent the winter in Paris, the home of his wife, Claire.

Back in 1898, already widely known through frequent reproductions of his works in journals such as *Die Jugend*, Christiansen was visited by Grand Duke Ernst Ludwig of Hesse in Paris, and became one of the first artist-professors to be called to Darmstadt. He was much in demand in Paris as a designer of stained-glass windows, posters, book illustrations as well as textiles, wallpaper, tableware, furniture and tapestries. During this period he continued to develop his painting as well. Gottorf Palace harbors not only many examples of Christiansen's glassware but also a number of his paintings, prints and designs, dating from 1891 to 1922.

Before going to Paris in 1893, Christiansen had completed training as a house painter, spent two years at the Munich School of Decorative Art and established his own decorative painting business in Hamburg. Like many other craftsmen of the day there, he was active in the city's Folk Art Association, which, in keeping with the Arts and Crafts Movement of the latter half of the nineteenth century, followed in the footsteps of William Morris and John Ruskin. In later years Christiansen maintained this contact, as he did with the Hamburg Association of Decorative Arts.

Hans Christiansen, Bruckmann and Sons, Heilbronn, ***set of silverware*** *(fifty-eight pieces), ca. 1901, silver, cast, partly gilt terminals, steel blades, l. 4 ⅝–13 in.*

This association, like the Museum of Arts and Crafts in the city on the Elbe, was largely shaped by Justus Brinckmann (1843–1915). In addition to establishing a department of Japanese art, Brinckmann defied the taste of the day by collecting plain china vessels, lacquerwork and examples of basketweaving. Among those on whose support he relied was Samuel Bing, an art dealer from Hamburg who a short time later logically changed the name of his Paris gallery from "Art Moderne" to "Art Nouveau."

Japanese color woodblock prints, and, from the middle of the 1890s, Japanese ceramics, soon formed the stylistic focus of the Hamburg Museum of Arts and Crafts, whose prime purpose was to instruct visually and develop taste among students of the decorative arts and working artisans. Brinckmann, along with his assistants Friedrich Deneken and Richard Stettiner, were key mediators in this regard. Thanks to the latter, in 1902, a friendship developed between Richard Mutz, a ceramicist who frequented the Japanese Department, and Ernst Barlach, a young artisan from Wedel, Holstein. Stettiner commissioned the two to create a plaque commemorating the 25th anniversary of the museum, in 1902, with which Brinckmann's contribution was honored.

Christiansen, too, owed the museum and its director much inspiration, including the encouragement to produce, in 1892, a book of ornamental patterns, *Neue Flachornamente.* This publication led to a revival of stencil painting and established a range of ornaments based on natural forms from which the artist himself would later profit, in the shape of his "Christiansen rose."

The Arts and Crafts Movement, its affiliated museums, schools, journals and the people involved, formed a dense network of relationships that continually contributed to the realization of innovative ideas. One of the institutions that relied essentially on this network was the school of weaving established in Scherrebek, north Schleswig, in 1896. The school was conceived principally as an instrument to further the Germanization of the Danish populace, in the context of the "Köller Policy," harsh and senseless measures named after their most zealous advocate, Ernst Mathias von Köller, Prussian president of the province from 1897 to 1901. Brinckmann, however, managed to use the school in the interest of German arts and crafts. His daughters Maria, Ida and Carlotta, all accomplished in the art of weaving, went to Scherrebek. Maria, repelled by the administration's nationalization policy, left the post of headmistress after only a few months and became a teacher of weaving at the Lette Association School in Berlin. Ida and Carlotta remained. Brinckmann's assistant, Deneken, a former fellow-student of Scherrebek's founder, Pastor Johannes Jacobsen, used his contacts to attract talent to the school. His friend Otto Eckmann provided designs for tapestries, as did such artists as Alfred Mohrbutter, Otto Ubbelohde, followed by Walter Leistikow and Henry van de Velde. Eckmann's designs of 1895 and 1896 formed the basis of Scherrebek school's production. *Smooth Passage* and *Flock of Seagulls* were the first tapestries made. Examples of both are now in the Schleswig-Holstein State Museums, as is the most famous Eckmann tapestry, *Five Swans* of 1896–97, which was produced in an edition of at least one hundred and was a resounding success both for the artist and the school.

*Otto Eckmann (1865–1902), **Smooth Passage**, 1896, Scherrebek weaving school, tapestry: linen warp, wool woof, 18 7/8 x 57 7/8 in.*

Like the preceding woodcuts *Two Swans* and *Three Swans* of 1895, the tapestry design reflects an involvement with Japanese woodblock prints, but also with Aubrey Beardsley's illustrations to Sir Thomas Malory's *Le Morte Darthur.* Acquired by museums and frequently reproduced, the tapestry soon became well-known, indeed famous; but it also prompted parodies. Heinrich Sperling, for instance, submitted tapestry designs featuring storks and pugdogs, which so deeply injured Eckmann that he resigned from his post in the school administration and refused all further cooperation. By then, thanks to his tapestry, the swan had become the heraldic bird of Art Nouveau, just as Christiansen's rose had become its emblem.

Otto Eckmann, ***Five Swans****, 1896–97, Scherrebek weaving school, tapestry hanging for a pillar, linen warp, wool woof, 93 ¾ x 27 ½ in.*

As contractually agreed, five complementary copies of *Five Swans* went to Pastor Jacobsen. After a brief heyday, including representation at the 1900 Paris World Fair, the weaving shop went bankrupt in 1903, and Jacobsen put his tapestries up for lottery. The fledgling Thaulow Museum in Kiel, the shop's earliest and most faithful client and predecessor of the Schleswig-Holstein State Museums Foundation, acquired one of these tapestries. It was destroyed by fire in World War II, but another copy was acquired for Gottorf Palace in 1978.

Scandinavian porcelain; furniture designed by Henry van de Velde, Peter Behrens and Richard Riemerschmid (which allude to other *Gesamtkunstwerke*); painting, furniture and crafts from the

Viennese Jugendstil movement, which found a home at the Hamburg School of Decorative Arts when such Viennese Secessionists as Franz Karl Dellavilla and Anton Kling were called there by Justus Brinckmann; numerous works by Wenzel Hablik, a student of Otto Hoffmann who was active as an interior designer in Itzehoe—the Art Nouveau Department gives a sense of the numerous variants of this style throughout Europe, from Vienna to Copenhagen. *MS*

“Things Belong to One Only Temporarily”: The Rolf Horn Foundation

With the Rolf Horn Foundation and the permanent exhibition of his collection since 1995, the landscape of art at Gottorf received a significant emphasis on works of classical modernism and abstract sculpture, which set striking accents in the Sculpture Park. When the Berlin entrepreneur, a native of Schleswig-Holstein, and his wife, Bettina, decided in 1988 to donate their collection to Gottorf Palace, it was in the knowledge that “things belong to you only temporarily.” Horn (1912–1995) was a collector and art patron, generous and enthusiastic, a donor who thought it quite natural to share his love of art with the public. Bettina Horn now runs the foundation in accordance with her husband’s wishes.

Horn enjoyed Gottorf Palace and its lovely island setting in the Schlei, the variety of its collections, the diversity of its buildings and, not least, the park with its ideal conditions for the presentation of sculpture. It was important for him to know that his art had found a haven in the state of his birth. Horn never lost contact with his northern German homeland—nor was his penchant for Emil Nolde a coincidence because, in his eyes, the northern German landscape was quintessentially embodied in this artist’s work.

It was a stroke of luck for Gottorf that the donor decided to further the reconstruction of one of its nineteenth-century stable buildings, in order to unite his collection with the museum’s Gallery of Classical Modernism under one roof. On commission from Horn, Jürg Steiner, a Swiss architect active in Berlin, converted the former Prussian military building into an exhibition space perfectly suited to its new purpose. The two erstwhile stables, each about 230 feet in length and totaling 18,300 square feet in area, now provide an aesthetically pleasing setting for paintings, sculptures and works on paper. Divided into a series of spacious rooms and intimate cabinets, the museum landscape consists of a combination of enclosed areas and intriguing views from one room to the next, the whole introduced by a foyer with museum shop and cafeteria.

The light and airy setting wonderfully complements the collection, which focuses on German Expressionism. The space is veritably pervaded by vibrant expressive force. It culminates in the work of Käthe Kollwitz (1867–1945). Her social commitment, captured in compelling imagery, had intrigued Horn as a boy at his home in Kiel. The same holds for Ernst Barlach (1870–1938), whose profound humanity and rigorous form deeply and lastingly moved the collector. Works by Kollwitz and Barlach accordingly form a key emphasis of the presentation. They are symbols of life, facets of committed or contemplative observation of the vicissitudes of human existence in which figures or heads convey messages of empathy. Their art is suffused by the necessity of stating, as Kollwitz put it, "what has by no means yet been sufficiently said."

To lend emotions expressive form, to depict realities invisible to the eye—that was the artistic credo of Emil Nolde (1867–1956). Nolde's painting, deeply rooted in his northern German origins, deals with both sensory and supersensory perceptions, invokes mystical forces and reflects his experiences of nature and life. Nolde's art is suffused by many yearnings, some that still move us today. It is no coincidence that his *Flower Garden P* of 1923 is the most popular painting in the Horn collection. One of the artist's most dazzlingly vital depictions of his garden, it conveys the act and substance of painting with great immediacy. The proliferation of red poppies speaks of the forces of nature and its beauty in this northern realm between land and sea. "Nolde, that ancient soul," said Paul Klee, "is more than just earthy—he is a demon of this region, too."

This lone wolf among the Expressionists is widely represented in the collection. In addition to watercolors with north Frisian motifs and a strikingly effective *Head of a Girl Wearing a Red Cap* (ca. 1920–25), there are two watercolor depictions titled *South Sea Islanders*, part of the yield of Nolde's travels in the South Pacific in 1913–14.

Back then, both Nolde and Max Pechstein, if each on a different path, made a pilgrimmage to the sources of modern art. The devel-

Emil Nolde (1867–1956), ***Flower Garden P****, 1923, oil on canvas, 28 ¾ x 34 ⅝ in., Rolf Horn Foundation*

opment of European art after 1900 was marked by a widespread fascination with art of the South Pacific and African sculpture. Examples were to be seen in the museums of ethnography that had begun to arise all over Europe by this period. Artists should go back to the "original beginnings of art, like those found in ethnographic collections," recommended Klee. And his view was shared by many artists of the day. Unsullied vitality and archaic, rigorous form—these qualities of "primitive art" were capable of helping Europeans overcome the constrictions of their society and broaden their intellectual horizon.

It is a fascination that has remained unbroken to this day. And a spark can leap the gap between the art of different worlds, as Rolf Horn realized when he saw the "Primitivism" exhibition held at the Museum of Modern Art, New York, and the influence it exerted on twentieth-century art. Horn found the show so overwhelming that it inspired him to extend his collecting activity to sub-Saharan and Oceanic sculpture. This provided the basis for the present dialogue at Gottorf between "primitive" sculpture and the art of Die Brücke—a confrontation of original imagery with its transformations into modern art of a range and depth found in few other museums in Germany.

Ibo, Nigeria, ***mask****, wood, white and black paint, h. 10 ⅞ in., Rolf Horn Foundation*

First priority of the artists who called themselves Die Brücke (The Bridge) was an art of unadulterated directness. Beginning in 1905, Ernst Ludwig Kirchner (1880–1938), Karl Schmidt-Rottluff (1884–1976), Erich Heckel (1883–1970), Max Pechstein (1881–1951) and Otto Mueller (1874–1930) developed a style of unleashed expressiveness that flew in the face of academic conventions. The work of these artists and their vital renewal hold an outstanding place in the Horn Foundation. Key examples include rare early woodcuts and portfolios, but also paintings of the 1920s and early 1930s (such as Kirchner's *Sertig Way* of 1924–25 and Mueller's *Landscape with Yellow Field* of 1923), which bear witness to the continuing elan and vitality of the Expressionist movement even after its adherents went their separate ways.

The early 1920s also saw the emergence of another, famous portfolio in the Horn collection: Max Beckmann's *Berlin Journey*, a series of ten lithographs that presents a kaleidoscopic view of an era in richly nuanced black and white. One of the major artists of the last century, Beckmann (1884–1950) went a lone and highly original way between empirical observation and expressive gesture, between realism and incipient abstraction.

Another solitary figure of the day was Christian Rohlfs (1849–1938), whose emblematic human images and depictions of the natural world relied on a strange, subdued palette and daring abbreviations of form. Rohlfs's canvases and woodcuts, largely done about 1920, reflect an ambivalent fantasy and melancholy magic unique in the art of the twentieth century as represented in the Horn collection.

Russian-born Alexei von Jawlensky (1864–1941) was likewise a highly independent modern artist. A former officer of the Imperial Guard, he initially developed his expressive style, a harmonious combination of luminous colors and powerful contours, in the company of the Munich artists' association Der Blaue Reiter (The Blue Rider). Our collection includes both oils and works on paper, which range from early, brilliantly hued depictions of women's heads to late, meditative ones, such as *Mosaic* of 1913, which features a woman's face resembling a stark icon. It was the Russians in Munich who provided food for thought, Franz Marc once wrote, and added, "Mysticism awakened in their souls and, with it, primeval elements of art."

Alexei von Jawlensky (1864–1941), ***Woman from Ascona****, 1917, oil on board, 19 5/8 x 6 3/4 in., Rolf Horn Foundation*

The slender stelae by Jan Koblasa (b. 1932) are like beings from an alien realm pervaded by magic forces, yet at the same time they are symbolic of the eternal presence of man. Born in Bohemia in 1932, Koblasa settled in Schleswig-Holstein in 1968. His stringent figures from the Horn collection are united with those from the Gottorf holdings in the Kreuzstall and Sculpture Park. They are like unearthly messengers of a silent melancholy,

*Bernhard Heiliger (1915–1995), **Tree between Two Worlds**, 1982, wrought iron, 63 x 236 1/4 x 102 3/8 in., Rolf Horn Foundation*

the creations of an artist who accepts no hard and fast borderline between figurative and non-objective art.

How strikingly effective contemporary sculptures can be in a landscape setting is shown especially by two pieces in the Sculpture Park: *Tree between Two Worlds* of 1982 and *Kronos* of 1983 by the Berlin sculptor Bernhard Heiliger (1915–1995). These large-scale, tension-filled, space-defining iron configurations were conceived for outdoor installation, and the historic backdrop of Gottorf Palace seems to heighten their effect of energy contained. Late in life, Rolf Horn grew increasingly enthusiastic about the idea of contrasting Heiliger's "constructed vitality," and sculptures by others of his generation, with landscaped park settings—so much so that he decided Gottorf would be the ideal place for these two sculptures. *UB*

Dancing on the Volcano and Images of Contemplation: The Georg Tappert Foundation

In 1925, at the apex of his artistic career and his activity as instructor at the State Art School in Berlin, Georg Tappert (1880–1957) painted two versions of *Carnival.* In the present version, an adolescent girl is depicted in festive makeup and mask, clad in an old-fashioned ball gown with a huge bow on the back. Holding a flower in her right hand and reticently crossing her left with it, she stands between two men, likewise in masks and wearing harlequin costumes. The flower is an araceae, from the arum family, and its form, recalling both phallus and vulva, obviously bears erotic connotations. The men seem older than the girl—or do their masks merely lend them an appearance of maturity? At any rate, they are approaching her with a certain lasciviousness, calling to mind the Old Testament story of Susanna and the Elders—a theme Tappert had already treated in an etching of 1916. Still, the reference remains vague, because unlike Susanna, this young woman shows no fear, seeming quite unconcerned with the men's presence or intentions. The inability of people to connect or relate to one another, a theme prevalent in modern art since Edouard Manet, has affected the protagonists of this picture as well, and in light of its overt erotic note, makes it a symbol of modern, big-city life.

Tappert experienced this life in his hometown of Berlin. He came of age in a period marked by the profound transitions of the Belle Epoque under the Kaiser to the Golden Twenties. After training at the Karlsruhe Academy and serving for a time as assistant to Paul Schultze-Naumburg at Saaleck Castle in southern Saxony-Anhalt, he began working in his early style, influenced by Art Nouveau. The years 1906 to 1909 accordingly found Tappert at a center of this movement, the artists' colony in Worpswede, where such friends as Heinrich Vogeler and Paula Modersohn-Becker encouraged him to pursue his work in the genres of portraiture, the nude, still-life and landscape painting. Tappert's teaching abilities also unfolded in Worpswede, and he established a private art school.

By 1909 he was back in Berlin, contributing to the development of an Expressionist approach out of Art Nouveau. When his work was rejected by the Berlin Secession, Tappert joined Max Pechstein and others in 1910 to found the New Secession, whose chairman he became. After serving for a time on the Western Front in World War I, Tappert was fortunate in being assigned a semi-civilian post in Berlin that permitted him to continue painting. After the war, he had contacts with the politically radical Left, but refused to adopt an extremist stance, apart from joining the hardline "Working Council

*Georg Tappert (1880–1957), **Carnival**, 1925, oil on canvas, 43 ¾ x 37 ¾ in., Georg Tappert Foundation*

for Art" in 1918. Yet more significant was Tappert's role as spokesman of the revolutionary "November Group," of which he, again with Pechstein, was cofounder. After his Expressionist beginnings, Tappert's ambition to remain at the forefront in the first postwar years led him, like Dix, to adopt Cubist and Futurist devices. He produced a series of facetted compositions with powerful rhythms and a brilliant palette.

A further fruitful and innovative phase followed, from 1922 to 1933. Now a recognized artist, Tappert grew increasingly confident and productive. In 1921 he was named professor at the State Art School, and the following year he became a member of the Art Review Board. Tappert also belonged to the board of the Deutscher Werkbund. In his paintings and drawings, an individual style combining expressive attack with faithfulness to reality now began to emerge. In the delirious Berlin of the 1920s, Tappert recorded a bourgeois society that was coming apart at the seams. Some of his models were women of the demimonde, whom he depicted in the

Georg Tappert, ***Portrait of the Artist's Father****, ca. 1909, oil on canvas, 30 ¾ x 30 ⅛ in., Georg Tappert Foundation*

nude with a drastic directness approaching that of a Dix or Grosz. The paint surfaces were extraordinarily sumptuous, celebrating the presence of the flesh, the sensuality of the female body, but also revealing an empathy for the human and social situation of his models.

The picture *Carnival* discussed above also contains a reference to Tappert's personal fate. In 1919 he had married an English woman, Kathleen Bagot, a talented artist and former student of his in Worpswede. Yet soon Tappert began an affair with another student, Elisabeth Foerstemann, and it was she whom he depicted as early as about 1921, masked and holding the phallic araceae. In the year *Carnival* was done, Kathleen suddenly died. Tappert married Elisabeth the following year. The artist may possibly have emotionally projected himself into the role of the young woman between two men in this painting. In 1929, Tappert lost his second wife, Elisabeth.

Although these strokes of fate deeply affected him personally, they lent Tappert's art greater depth and seriousness. He found fulfillment in his teaching activity and was admired by his many students, whose individual talents he sensitively furthered. Tappert made no attempt to influence their development in the direction of his own approach. This is why such diverse artists emerged from his classes as Wilhelm Morgener (from the Worpswede period), Ernst Strassner (from the 1920s in Berlin) and Bernard Schultze (from the mid-1930s).

Just a few weeks after Hitler rose to power, Tappert began to feel the effects of Nazi persecution. A group of SA students kicked in the door of his studio at the art college. Not only an Expressionist artist but a committed socialist, Tappert could not help but attract the wrath of the new regime. He was rapidly forced out of his teaching post, first temporarily, then permanently. His art was declared "degenerate" and he was forbidden to work.

This persecution proved to be a blow from which the sensitive fifty-three-year-old artist was never to recover. Initially he withdrew into himself, painting barren landscapes devoid of human life, some of them extremely effective. Yet under the pressure of events, Tappert had entirely ceased to paint by the time war broke out.

After 1945 he was reinstated in his position at the College of Art Education. As an educator he was instrumental, with Karl Hofer and Heinrich Ehmsen, in establishing the new Berlin Art Academy (Hochschule für bildende Künste), which had merged with the College. Hofer became first director, Tappert second. Yet despite this recognition, Tappert was never entirely able to overcome the persecution he had suffered. His later wife, Annalise Friedrich, supported him during these troubled times, and shared in his recognition as an educator. Yet Tappert was never to paint again.

*Georg Tappert, **Farm in the Dunes near Keitum**, ca. 1939, oil on canvas, 24 1/4 x 27 1/2 in., Georg Tappert Foundation*

The fact that a review of his oeuvre was to be seen in a memorial exhibition mounted in Berlin in 1958, only a year after his death, stood opposed to Tappert's place in art history. The history of modern art had seemingly already been written, without reference to Tappert, whose work was as good as unknown. Accordingly an attempt was made to define his oeuvre in terms of the established concepts, which initially did violence to it. Yet soon more careful attention was paid by art historians and the trade to the forgotten artist, which, following the numerous works by Gerhard Wietek, culminated in a monograph published on the anniversary of his 100th birthday, in 1980. This did justice to Tappert's achievement and ensured him a distinguished place in the history of twentieth-century art.

The Tappert Foundation has been located at Gottorf Palace since 1995. Annalise Tappert, at the recommendation of Wietek, donated her husband's estate, consisting of about two hundred paintings, several thousand drawings, watercolors and prints, as well as the glass negative plates of his photographs. Works from the Georg Tappert Foundation have been presented in a series of exhibitions at Gottorf Palace and published in stock catalogues. *TG*

Sculpture by Hans Wimmer: The Studio

The estate of Hans Wimmer, generously donated to our museum by his family in 1993, includes not only the entire equipment of his studio but over one hundred original casting models, representing almost a quarter of the artist's surviving oeuvre. Beyond this, preparatory maquettes and studies from over five decades provide documentary material, which, in terms of completeness and authenticity, is probably unmatched by that relating to any other German sculptor of the twentieth century.

Hans Wimmer (1907–1992), ***Portrait of Ernst Jünger****, 1972, original plaster model, h. 13 3/8 in., three bronzes were cast*

One of the most important genres in Wimmer's oeuvre is portraiture, for which he became known early in his career. His portraits are characterized not only by likeness, but by a high degree of psychological penetration of the sitters' characters and a translation of physical appearances into compelling aesthetic form.

Wimmer's portrait of Wilhelm Furtwängler was executed in 1953, a year before the conductor and composer's death, in Rome, where he was conducting Wagner's *Ring of the Nibelung* for Italian radio. In advance of the portrait sittings, Wimmer was able to observe and

Hans Wimmer, ***Portrait of Wilhelm Furtwängler,*** *1953, original plaster model, h. 17 ⅝ in., three bronzes were cast*

sketch Furtwängler during rehearsals. These primarily full-figure "working sketches," published in 1954, reflect the sculptor's concern with capturing the entire personality of those he depicted. The ensuing sculptural portrait shows the conductor deeply immersed in the music, his eyes closed, his forehead furrowed as if to shut out the outside world. The face is an embodiment of creative concentration, of an intense listening to an inward conception of orchestral harmonies.

Wimmer looked upon Oskar Kokoschka as a "visionary foremost." His portrait of his fellow artist focuses on the eyes, around whose penetrating gaze the other facial features are centered. Like the massive nose, the eyes are emphasized, in fact modeled in an almost exaggerated way. Yet the intensity of the gaze, which seems directed through and beyond the external world toward some inner image, not only speaks of the visionary who set out to open people's eyes with his "school of seeing." The portrait also evokes self-doubt and the restlessness of Kokoschka's never-ending search, as in the inclination of the head or the unsmoothed surface, in which every trace of the working process is still to be seen.

Wimmer's friendship with Kokoschka went back to the period shortly after World War II. His portrait head of the eighty-one-year-

Hans Wimmer, ***Oskar Kokoschka,*** *1967, original plaster model, h. 12 ⅜ in., three bronzes were cast*

old painter was done in 1967, after a protracted stay with the Kokoschkas in Villeneuve.

The previous year, 1966, saw Wimmer portraying Aba, the lovely African lady who had come to Munich with Carl Orff. Done as an "ideal portrait," not by order but solely out of admiration for Aba's beauty, the bust is a perfect example of Wimmer's striving for an ideal that transcended individual appearances.

Proud as a queen, holding her head with its elongated crown of hair erect, this woman exudes an overwhelming physical presence that reflects an unbroken sense of her own body. She gazes out at the viewer through large, clear eyes under narrow brows. The same self-confidence is conveyed by the nostrils, which seem almost to breathe, and the full lips. Above narrow but powerful shoulders rises a long slender neck; the curve of the collarbones echoes those of the firm upper arms and full breasts. The physiognomical details have been worked out with well-nigh unprecedented care. The painstakingly rendered features and the large crown of hair, but especially the expression of pride and dignity, recall ancient Egyptian sculpture, despite the fact that similarly striking coiffures are also found in African art. It is indicative of Wimmer's work that Egyptian references outweigh those to "primitive" art.

Hans Wimmer, ***Aba: "La belle Africaine"****, 1966, bronze, h. 21 ¾ in., third cast of the first version*

His careful observation stands in contrast to an aura that commands a respectful distance and at the same time conveys the foreignness of *La belle Africaine*, a foreignness that is not exhibited as charming exoticism but evokes a different, strange and inaccessible world.

Wimmer's receptiveness to feminine beauty is also reflected in his reclining *Desdemona*. He completed the piece in 1976, after having toyed for years with the idea of doing a reclining figure. In 1969 he had addressed the up-to-date theme of a young, reclining mannequin, producing a figurine that quite transcended the contemporary context. Years later Wimmer finally found a model for a reclining figure that put "wind in my sails," as he told fellow artist Gerhard Marcks. The point of departure, in other words, was not the literary motif but observation of nature. The title *Desdemona* was given to the figure after the fact, inspired above all by the eloquence of the reclining motif. The figure's head has sunken, eyes closed, to her shoulder. Her right arm, resting on a stone, dangles helplessly. Only the left hand still contains a hint of the relaxing tension that suffuses the arm lying almost outstretched on the hip. A stringently composed, harmonious lineature runs through the entire sculpture, creating the effect of an endless outflow of energy, which is expressed as much in the movement of the comprehensive volumes as in the projection of the limbs into all three dimensions of space.

Beyond its literary content, the true subject of the figure is mortality as a basic condition of human existence—and as the fundamental condition of that beauty of which we become fully aware only in the face of death.

Being a passionate rider, Wimmer devoted special attention to the subject of horses. They not only represented a sculptural challenge to him, but embodied the power of a creature that nevertheless permits itself to be made useful to man.

By comparison to his previous depictions of horses, Wimmer's *Saddled Horse* of 1952–58 is more calm, contained and formally stringent. Its head raised, the animal stands quiet and relaxed on legs, each of which bears equal weight and is slightly shifted toward the mid-

Hans Wimmer, ***Saddled Horse****, 1952–58, original plaster model, 31 x 28 ½ x 9 in., six versions were cast in bronze*

dle. The details are observed with almost portrait-like fidelity, as in the finely modeled head. Yet they are still subordinated to the overall compositional scheme, as in the pinned-back ears, which normally signal aggressive readiness. The theme of a saddled but riderless horse, especially in combination with the unusual leg position, would seem to be predicated on a knowledge of Chinese horse sculptures of the Tang Dynasty. Here we find the same well-nigh ornamental condensation of natural forms into a sculpturally concise configuration with a clear, curving contour—an inspiration Wimmer combines with a solid tectonics based on bone structure. Strikingly, the horse is depicted with a light riding saddle but without bridle or reins. Apart from aesthetic considerations, this likely reflects Wimmer's respect for the "personality" of the animal, which is evoked in a veritably monumental way.

In *Biga* of 1984–91, a life-size, two-horse team driven by a female charioteer, the two central themes of Wimmer's work are combined in a monument that reflects his admiration for the art of antiquity. Yet in contrast to Greco-Roman tradition, his charioteer cannot be interpreted to represent a goddess, for neither the tranquil composition of the group nor the low, earthbound pedestal contains triumphal elements. In accordance with the rigorously axial symmetry of the whole, the figure of the charioteer is treated in a strict, statuesque way. In the case of the horses, subtle nuances can be detected despite the tendency to unification of effect, indicating that Wimmer never lost sight of the living model. Nevertheless, *Biga* conveys the impression of an ideal, an expression of the artist's admiration for women and love of horses merged into a single, unified image, in which Wimmer's life and life's work are embodied as if in a keystone.

UK

The Charm of Diversity: Modern Crafts and Design in the Kreuzstall

Manufactured products shaped by an artist's hand—what is generally known as industrial design—have become so much a part of our everyday lives that we rarely give them a second thought. This was not the case in the 1920s and 1930s, the heyday of the Bauhaus. This art school, founded in Weimar, would fundamentally influence the history of design—and the beginnings of mass production.

Among the classics that emerged from the Bauhaus was the "Free Swinger" by Marcel Breuer (1902–1981), which is still being manufactured today. Fabricated of cold-drawn and bent steel tubing, the chair has a springy feeling to it that gave rise to its name. In the original version seen here, the canvas consists of a heavy-duty weave. Logic of construction and functionality were the focus of all Breuer's furniture designs. In his desk, for instance, the top, chest of drawers and surface on the right are designed as separate elements and linked only by the steel-tube framework. The visual appeal of the piece is inseparable from its function. Its decor is limited to bakelite knobs and keyholes in a contrasting color. These contrasts of material and color (black—red—silver) were typical of the Bau-

*Marcel Breuer (1902–1981), Thonet, Vienna, **"B 33" Chair ("Free Swinger") and "B 327" Desk**, 1927–28 and 1932, chair: chrome-plated tubular steel and canvas, desk: tubular steel, ebonized wood, bakelite, 33 ⅛ x 19 x 24 in. and 28 ⅞ x 69 ½ x 31 ½ in.*

haus artists' aesthetic. In place of cozy comfort, they took the cool straightforwardness of technical industrial products as their ideal of interior design.

Breuer had been a student at the Bauhaus. From 1925 to 1928 he headed the furniture workshop there, and concerned himself with applying the entirely new material of steel tubing to furniture. The resulting prototypes were already in use at the Dessau Bauhaus by 1925–26. In 1929, Breuer's steel-tube furniture went into series production at the Thonet Company, whose nineteenth-century bentwood chairs had become incunabula of modern furniture design.

Apart from the Bauhaus, international design received important impulses from Scandinavia in the 1930s. A key figure here was the Finnish architect and designer Alvar Aalto (1898–1976), whose work exerted a lasting influence not only in Germany but also in the United States. The "Savoy" vase is one of Aalto's most famous designs for serial production. A number of variants in different forms and sizes exist. The decisive feature is the wavelike contour, which extends over the entire surface, engendering light reflections that bring the vessel to life. Created in 1936 for a glass design competition held by the Littala Company, where it won first prize, this vase is still being successfully manufactured by the same company today.

Characteristic of Aalto's style are organic forms. These also figure in his laminated wood furniture, various examples of which are on view in our collection. Aalto succeeded in combining functional simplicity with flowing, natural configurations. Although he was influenced by the constructive Bauhaus style, he gave his designs more of a human than a technological aspect.

A gifted countryman of Aalto's was Tapio Wirkkala (1915–1985). He was known especially as a glass designer, and several pieces in our collection illustrate why this was so. Wirkkala also wrote design history with his designs for the German porcelain manufacturer Rosenthal. On the occasion of its one-hundred-year jubilee, in 1979, Rosenthal premiered Wirkkala's service "Century." It exists in white and decorated versions. In 1982 the shape of the handles was altered, as seen in the service on exhibit. The surface texture of the pieces recalls the Chinese rice-grain pattern, and their walls, unusually thin for modern porcelain, likewise have an Asian touch. Originally the surface was planned to have a pattern in low relief, but for practical reasons—ease of cleaning—it was embossed instead.

Other artists have replied to burgeoning technology and automation by focusing on one-off designs. A prime example are modern artists' ceramics, which are well represented in our collection. These include three small works from the early period of Jan Bontjes van Beek (1899–1969), one of Germany's major ceramicists. Bontjes van Beek, whose parents came from Holland, spent his first years as a potter in the village of Fischerhude, an artists' colony outside Bremen.

Jan Bontjes van Beek (1899–1969), ***small round vase, tea caddy and bowl,*** *1925–43, stoneware, manganese earthenware, earthenware with various glazes, vase: h. 3 ¼ in., tea caddy: h. 30 ⅜ in., bowl: diam. 5 ⅜ in.*

He maintained close contacts with the art scene in nearby Worpswede as well. In 1933 Bontjes van Beek moved to Berlin.

The plain forms and thick overglazes of his pieces, such as the small, round vase shown here, reveal affinities with French Art Nouveau ceramics. Yet the expressive, contrast-rich glazed decor goes far beyond that of earlier styles. Bontjes van Beek was especially interested in glazes and, although he employed a potter to turn the vessels he designed, he applied the glazes himself, experimenting with various effects in a small kiln specially reserved for the purpose. As with many other European potters, an involvement with Far Eastern and especially Chinese ceramics was fundamental to the development of Bontjes van Beek's style. His works are characterized by the eschewal of superfluous detail and the sensuous, occasionally meditative effect of the glazes. In the 1950s and 1960s, Bontjes van Beek achieved great international recognition and lastingly influenced German ceramics, as exemplified by the work of such talents as Karl and Ursula Scheid.

A key ensemble in the collection of northern European ceramics is formed by works from the Kiel School of Ceramics. Founded by Johannes Gebhardt (b. 1930), the school now enjoys a reputation far beyond Schleswig-Holstein's borders. Gebhardt's vessel-objects of the 1980s, delicate and recalling flower calyxes, were succeeded by heavy, irregularly shaped vessels, such as the Stone Sphere. Like this piece, the Spherical Vessels were inspired by naturally occuring forms. Their massive walls, dark slip and seemingly random surface texture put one in mind of stones or lava formations. In contrast to the vegetal configurations of earlier phases, however, the formal reduction of Gebhardt's Stone Sphere draws attention to the material, whose elemental presence is underscored. This makes it a characteristic transition work to the architectural ceramic objects of the artist's recent years.

Karl Scheid (b. 1929), ***two vases****, 1993 and 1990, stoneware, feldspar-based glaze, h. 10 3/8 in. and 8 in.*

From 1956 onward, Gebhardt served as head of the ceramics class at the Muthesius-Werkkunstschule in Kiel. Until his retirement in 1994, he taught a series of potters who have since made names for themselves, and whose work is likewise well represented in the museum's collection.

The large, brilliant blue bowl by Alev Ebüzziya-Siesbye (b. 1938) is a particularly striking example of our extensive collection of contemporary Danish ceramics, which have found acclaim far beyond the country's borders. Ebüzziya-Siesbye's artistic background and activity are truly international. Born in Istanbul, she studied ceramics and sculpture at the local academy, then moved to Germany. In 1963, she settled in Copenhagen, where she maintained a studio until 1988. Since then she has lived and worked in Paris.

Alev Ebüzziya-Siesbye (b. 1938), ***large bowl****, 1986, stoneware with lapis lazuli glaze, h. 9 7/8 in., diam. 15 1/2 in.*

Ebüzziya-Siesbye's one-off pieces, which now fetch high prices, are based on configurations of ceramics in her Turkish homeland. Out of a combination of luminous color and tense, projecting form, her large blue bowl develops an effect that is veritably aura-like. This is further heightened by the vessel's extremely narrow base ring.

Gerda Regina Moll (b. 1940), ***necklace,*** *1987, sterling silver and white gold, diam. 6 3/4 in.*

Delicate decor, derived from unglazed passages that leave the basic material visible, is a further mark of Ebüzziya-Siesbye's ceramics. In contrast to the brilliant blue of the glaze, the light, fine-textured clay in the narrow ornamental band comes wonderfully into play.

In addition to handmade, one-off pieces, the artist has designed services for serial production at the Royal Porcelain Factory in Copenhagen and for Rosenthal in Germany, which are also on view in the exhibition.

When it comes to the great range of creations by the region's contemporary goldsmiths and jewelry designers, mention can be made of only a few, key representatives. These include Gerda Regina and Wilfried Moll, a husband-and-wife goldsmith team of Hamburg. While Wilfried Moll designs silverware and services for large production runs, his wife concentrates on unique pieces of jewelry, such as the sterling silver and white gold necklace illustrated here. The piece is marked by a tense interplay of transparency and plasticity. Convex chased rectangles of silver—triangular versions also exist—soldered together in pairs form the basic elements. The intrinsic effect of the fine metal is accentuated by the delicate links of white gold wire. Gerda Regina Moll is concerned with the balanced proportions of the individual elements that form a harmonious whole. Characteristic of her jewelry is a subtle rhythm that is engendered by the interplay of positive and negative shapes. This is found not only in her necklaces but also in her rings, bracelets and earrings—as well as in the non-utilitarian "cushion objects," two of which are in our collection.

How permeable the borders are between applied and fine art, becomes especially evident in the field of textiles. German tapestry design of the twentieth century was materially shaped by the formative influence of educational institutions in the northern part of the country, beginning with the Scherrebek weaving school, a pilot project, founded in 1896 (see p. 74). The art of weaving and tapestry-making found a further culmination at the Bauhaus, in whose tradition an artist such as Thyra Hamann-Hartmann stands—in terms not of the design for mass production propagated there, but of the stylistic influences carried by Bauhaus artists throughout the world.

Hamann-Hartmann began her training in 1939, at the Krefeld School of Textile Engineering. Her teacher was Georg Muche, who had headed the Bauhaus weaving department from 1921 to 1927. In Berlin, she also took instruction in painting from Oskar Moll, a student of Matisse, which visibly influenced her style. The subtle color gradations, multiple refractions and atmospheric density of her landscapes possess an expressiveness that is veritably painterly in effect.

In the 1960s, the artist's geometrically stringent Bauhaus style began to give way to freer, more fluid forms, and the lucid colors were supplemented by more delicate, pastel and mixed tones. Landscape depictions were accompanied by more abstract compositions, among which *Eastern Composition I* of 1970 holds an outstanding place. Spread over a patterned beige ground is a delicate web of nearly transparent-looking blended hues of light gray, light blue, light green and light salmon pink, whose center is marked by more intense colors and a variety of more condensed forms.

The force and freshness of Hamann-Hartmann's tapestries derive largely from the fact that she works on the upright loom not from full-sized designs but from small compositional sketches. This permits a spontaneous choice and combination of diverse color gradations and materials during the weaving process, thus becoming a further source of inspiration. *CK and UK*

The Palace as Residence of the Dukes of Schleswig-Holstein-Gottorf

The earliest record of a building on Palace Island dates from 1161, when Bishop Occo of Schleswig had a palace erected at this strategically important site. In 1268 the palace passed to the Dukes of Schleswig by way of exchange. Remnants of the original palace have survived to this day, for instance parts of the mighty ring fortification in the masonry of Gottorf Palace. A crucial chapter in the history of the region began in the year 1460, when the King of Denmark, Christian I

Anonymous master, ***Duke Adolf of Schleswig-Holstein-Gottorf****, 1586, oil on canvas, 48 ½ x 36 ½ in., on loan from the Museum für Hamburgische Geschichte, Hamburg*

of Oldenburg, was elected by the local nobility to Duke of Schleswig and Count (later Duke) of Holstein (Treaty of Ripen). This brought Gottorf into his possession.

His son, Frederick I, retained Gottorf as his principal residence, even after he became King of Denmark in 1523. His reign saw construction measures that still determine the look of the palace today. After a great fire in 1492, Frederick built the two-aisle Gothic Hall, which presumably served as an assembly room. In the seventeenth century it harbored the renowned Gottorf Library, to which the signs of the zodiac on the vaulting still attest.

About 1530, Frederick I had a west wing added to the palace. This annex, known as the Neues Haus, is a major work of the Early Renaissance in northern Europe and a truly royal palace. Its brick masonry is punctuated by architectural decor in freestone. The center of interest is a richly adorned projecting bay, which, on account of its numerous windows, is known as the "lantern." In its present state, it represents a reconstruction of the 1980s into which many original fragments were incorporated.

The birth of the Dukedom of Scheswig-Holstein-Gottorf is generally dated to the year 1544, when King Christian III of Denmark, son of Frederick I, decided to share his rule over the Dukedoms of Schleswig and Holstein with his brothers, John the Elder and Adolf. The youngest brother, Adolf (1526–1586), who came of age that year, chose what was known as the Gottorf portion, named for its main palace.

The legal construction of the parts of the region in both dukedoms ruled over by Adolf was intricate, however, and contained the seed of later conflicts. As Duke of Schleswig, Adolf was in fief to his brother and coregent, Christian III of Denmark. In addition, a treaty of union with Denmark obligated the duke of Gottorf to maintain peace and friendship. As Duke of Holstein, on the other hand, Adolf held the title of prince directly subject to the Holy Roman Empire of the German Nation. From 1548 to 1553, Adolf served as imperial commander at the court of Charles V, traveled to the imperial cities of Augsburg and Cologne, and above all to the Netherlands. Upon returning to the dukedoms, Adolf succeeded in considerably expanding his territory, especially through the capture of the rich peasant republic of Dithmarschen in 1559. During the subsequent period he concentrated on consolidating his realm, for instance by installing a central administration at Gottorf with a "modern" chancery and competent—that is, university-educated—advisers of burgher origin.

The expansion and consolidation of his power was reflected not least in Adolf's extensive additions and reconstructions, intended to demonstrate his ducal sway over all areas of his territory. Many changes were made, especially at the palace. After a terrible fire on

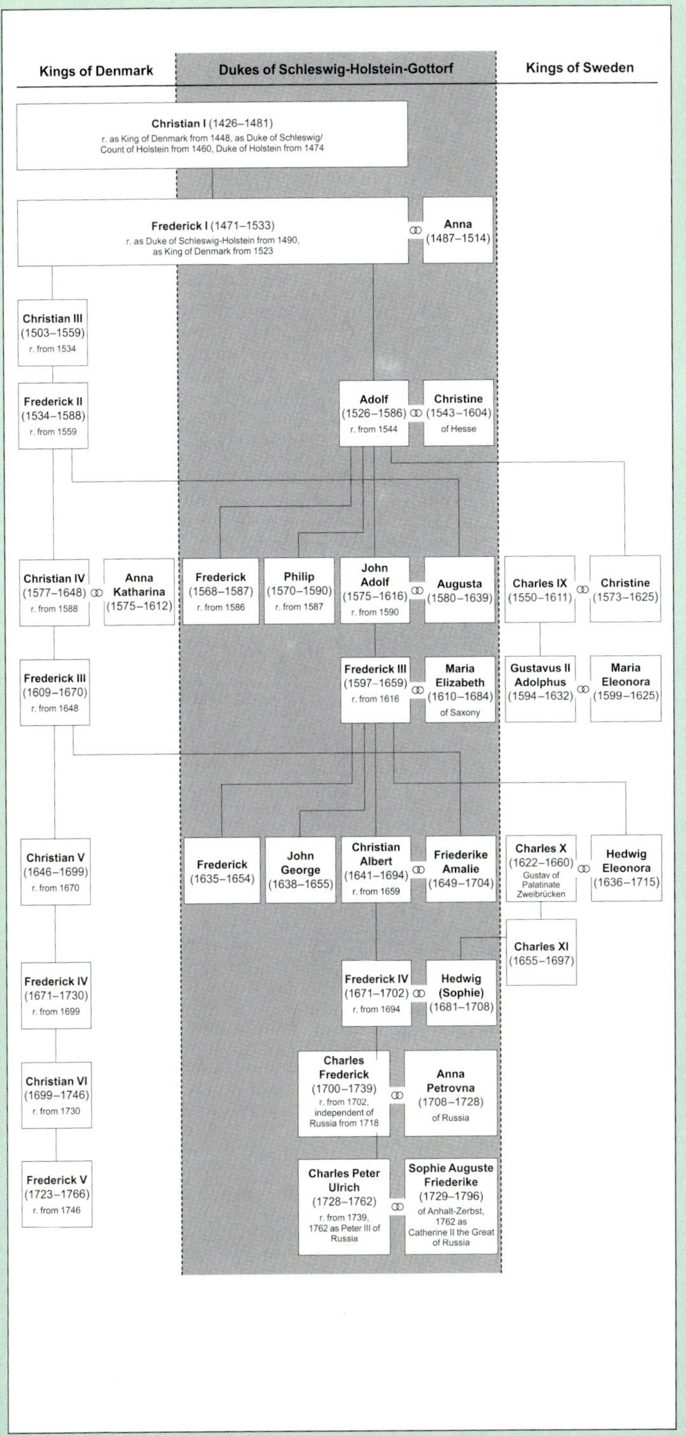

The Gottorf dukes and their dynastic interrelationships

Gothic Hall, built ca. 1500, containing sculptures dating from the 13th to the 15th century

· ***Palace Chapel*** *with original furnishings from the 1590s and the Ducal Oratory (1610–14)*

The Ducal Oratory with sumptuous intarsias and ornamental woodwork by the court cabinetmaker Andreas Salgen and woodcarver Jürgen Gower

New Year's night in 1564–65, the east wing was expanded into the courtyard by arcades or open galleries (which today are no longer visible), and toward the end of Adolf's reign, he had the north wing rebuilt. These building projects were subsequently continued by his sons Frederick II, Philip and John Adolf in particular. On the whole, Adolf left to his heirs a solidly established state with an early modern administration whose territory had grown to double that of 1544.

Since Duke Adolf's two eldest sons, Frederick II and Philip, died shortly after one another (in 1587 and 1590), the ducal title passed to his third son, John Adolf (1575–1616). His regency brought peace and further interior consolidation to the region. It also brought an increase of power with respect to the local nobility, a power that now extended to areas formerly under the sway of the church, such as schools, care for the sick and poor, as well as the judiciary and trade organizations.

Early Baroque organ front (ca. 1567) with case

***Deer Hall** (Hirschsaal), completed in 1595, with life-size stucco reliefs of deer*

set against a painted background of picturesque landscapes

Relations with Denmark culminated in John Adolf's marriage to Augusta, sister of the Danish queen, in the year 1596. The duke was also able to make successful matches for his daughters, which furthered the integration of Gottorf in the ranks of European royal houses.

The need for an outward expression of this position grew accordingly. John Adolf finished construction on the north wing, whose magnificence is still reflected today in the chapel and the Deer Hall (Hirschsaal), a Renaissance banqueting hall with life-size stucco reliefs of deer and stags adorning the walls. In the 1610s, the duke had a heatable private oratory built into the chapel (see pp. 106, 126), featuring the Royal Danish coat of arms of Duchess Augusta facing the chapel hall. The room had the atmosphere of an intimate parlor, and was decorated with fine intarsias and other ornamental woodwork. The coarse, feudal traits of life at court gave way to a greater refinement, as John Adolf began to further music and the arts and sciences. The establishment of the famous Gottorf Library as an institution, in 1606, was a high point in this development.

Frederick III was only nineteen when he succeeded his father in 1616. In him the sciences, especially mathematics and astronomy, and the visual and musical arts found a great patron, who transformed the Gottorf court into a northern European cultural center of the first rank. Frederick's court scholar, polymath Adam Olearius, was responsible for the ducal collections, the library, the numismatic collection and the Gottorf *Kunstkammer*, founded in 1650. Olearius published a series of significant writings at the Schleswig Court Printing Office. But above all, he worked out the plans for the renowned Gottorf Globe and "Sphaera Copernicana."

Even though few traces of his reign are now visible at Gottorf Palace, Frederick III devoted considerable effort to improving his residence. As Danckwerth reported in 1652, "at the palace, nothing particular was built, until ... our present reigning most gracious prince and lord came to power; since then, H.R.H. has not only had everything that was necessary repaired, but especially has had almost all the chambers, particularly his own, the Cabinet and the lovely, long Dance Hall, wonderfully decorated and gradually completely

The following two double-page spreads:
***Two rooms in the north wing**, the vaulting of which is adorned with 17th-century stuccowork attributed to Georg Ritteln. Frederick III commissioned the stuccowork after 1624. This suite of Baroque rooms culminates in the blue room, which has been graced with that color since the early neoclassical period. The stuccowork has a sculptural character and depicts idyllic town- and landscapes with castles. The blue room, which must originally have served the dukes as a guest room, affords a fine view of the Globe House and the terrace garden. Today the room provides the ideal setting in which to display the work of Gottorf's court painter, Jürgen Ovens (1623–1678), and contemporary furniture.*

furnished, as all now essentially stands, and is pleasurably looked upon by strangers...."

Today, an idea of the residence's former splendor is conveyed only by the surviving fine stuccowork in the duke's private chamber, the Frederick III Hall, and a series of rooms in the north wing. The furnishings were once enriched by valuable Gobelins and gilded leather wall coverings from the Netherlands, but above all by exquisite silk textiles from Persia. The latter were a gift of the Shah of Per-

Julius von Strachen (active 1638–48), ***Duke Frederick III of Schleswig-Holstein-Gottorf****, ca. 1640–45, oil on canvas, 85 x 52 ¾ in.*

The ducal apartment, comprising three rooms adorned with stuccowork dating from the same period, was located on the first floor of the west and previously

*adjoining south wing. What survives is the **Frederick III Hall** in the west wing, today used to exhibit a fine collection of Kellinghusen faience.*

sia, brought to Schleswig by his emissary in 1639. This visit was a reply to a Gottorf expedition to Persia, which, though it did not result in the hoped-for economic success—participation in the profitable silk trade—did have a highly significant scientific and cultural yield. The *Moscowitische und Persianische Reisebeschreibung*, a description of the expedition by Olearius, who accompanied it as secretary, was translated into many languages and has remained to this day a standard reference work on Russia and Persia in the seventeenth century. This great and audacious expedition of the 1630s was all the more remarkable for occuring during the Thirty Years' War, whose effects the dukedom began to feel when the king of Denmark entered it.

In reaction to these events, as well as to the shift of power in northern Europe in favor of Sweden, Frederick III pursued a policy of rapprochement with Sweden, which was officially sealed with the marriage of his daughter Hedwig Eleonora to King Charles X Gustav. In 1658, at the peace negotiations at Roskilde between the rivals Sweden and Denmark, the duke, with Swedish support, achieved a rescindment of Denmark's feudal tenure over Gottorf. However, Frederick III was not destined to see Gottorf's sovereignty confirmed in 1660, in the Treaty of Copenhagen. He died on August 10, 1659, at Tönning Bastion, where he had been forced to retire during the conflict.

In 1660, when Frederick's third son, Duke Christian Albert, succeeded to the title, Gottorf was at the apex of its power. Following his father's advice, Christian Albert attempted to maintain friendly relations with Denmark while entering protective alliances with Sweden. In 1667 he married Princess Friederike Amalie of Denmark, not lastly in the hope of being able to serve as mediator between the two Scandinavian powers. With the accession of Christian V to the Danish throne in 1670, however, a repressive policy toward Gottorf began that rapidly undermined their relations. An ally of powerful France, Christian V conducted a reunification policy along French lines. He repeatedly occupied Gottorf territory, forcing Christian Albert to go into exile in Hamburg (1675–79 and 1684–89). Gottorf came under the wheels of European power politics and became dependent on the changing alliances of the great powers. Yet thanks to Swedish intervention, Christian Albert was reinstated in his rights in 1689, and was able to return to Gottorf.

In view of these events, his cultural ambitions were all the more laudable. In 1665, Christian Albert was able to found the university in Kiel that his father had envisioned. But, above all, he completed the layout of the Baroque Neuwerk Garden north of the palace, with its magnificent terraces crowned, as a *point de vue*, by Amalienburg, a pleasure seat named after his wife. Christian Albert's premature death in 1694 put an abrupt end to further construction, as it did to his policy of rapprochement with Denmark.

The rule of Frederick IV brought a turnabout in Gottorf policy. He had spent his boyhood at the Stockholm court and—despite an obligation to maintain neutrality—openly expressed his enmity toward Denmark. In 1698, Frederick IV was named generalissimo of Sweden, a post that went hand in hand with massive military armament, with an eye to playing the role of auxiliary power in the concert of the greats.

Frederick IV's high-flown plans as an ally of Sweden included an extensive conversion of Gottorf, begun in 1699. He ordered the old south wing, except for the Gothic Hall, completely rebuilt and expanded eastward. The great south tower was demolished and rebuilt several feet farther on, at the center of the south wing. The strict axial symmetry of the resulting High Baroque facade was visible expression of the duke's absolutist claims. Yet Frederick IV was not to experience the completion of the south wing, nor the abandonment

David von Krafft (1655–1724), ***Duke Frederick IV of Schleswig-Holstein-Gottorf****, ca. 1700, oil on canvas, 52 x 41 3/4 in.*

of all further expansion plans. In service as generalissimo of Sweden, he fell in the Battle of Klezow, in Poland, in 1702.

Trustee government for his two-year-old son, Charles Frederick, went to Frederick IV's brother, Christian August, who continued the policy of confrontation with Denmark. In 1713, the Danish King Frederick IV took a breach of the neutrality oath as reason to reoccupy Schleswig and seize it as a fiefdom. The defeat of Sweden in the Great Northern War of 1721 sealed the incorporation of the dukedom in the Danish empire, leaving the Duke of Gottorf only remnants of his former territory, including portions of Holstein.

Gottorf Palace became the seat of the Danish governor; its entire inventory, including its valuable collections, were removed to Copenhagen beginning in 1734. In 1848–50, after the Schleswig-Holstein Uprising, the palace was converted into a hospital and then a Danish barracks; following the war with Prussia in 1864, it became a Prussian barracks. The Baroque fortifications were razed, the auxiliary buildings demolished. They were replaced by cavalry facilities, such as the Kreuzstall and Reithalle, horse stables and exercise hall, which were later converted to harbor portions of the museum's collections.

UK

A Historical Tour Given in the Order in which the Exhibition Rooms are Arranged

Middle Ages
Renaissance

Models
Baroque and
Baroque
Garden

Palace Chapel
High Baroque

Rococo
Neoclassicism
Biedermeier
Art Nouveau

Folk Art
Iron Age
Ethnology

Nydam Boat
Twentieth-Century Art

Ground Floor

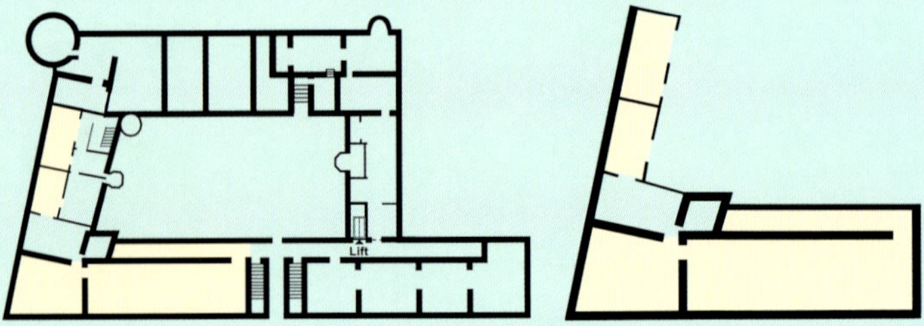

The section on art and culture of the **Middle Ages** contains objects relating to the ecclesiastical history of the state of Schleswig-Holstein, from the Romanesque to the Late Gothic period. Altarpieces and sculptures of the thirteenth to fifteenth centuries are exhibited in the Gothic Hall, built about 1500.

In a separate room, furniture and tableware provide an impression of everyday life in the late Middle Ages. Precious implements, chalices and the Rendsburg fragment of the Gutenberg Bible are found in the ecclesiastical treasury.

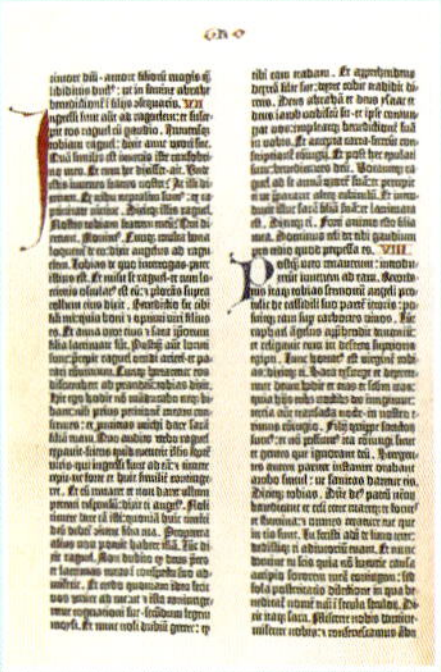

Ground Floor

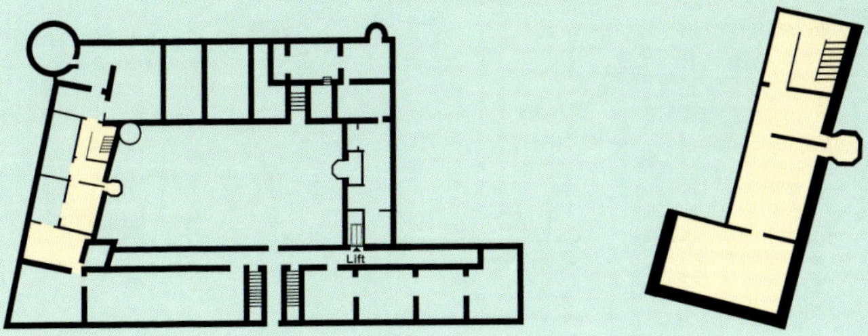

Paintings by Lucas Cranach and his workshop are a special emphasis in the collections on the art and culture of the **Renaissance**. In quantity and quality they are on a par with the former Cranach collection that had come to Gottorf with Duchess Maria Elizabeth of Saxony in 1630. Paintings by Netherlandish masters and tapestries, furniture and valuable tableware provide a vivid impression of the aristocratic way of life in the Renaissance.

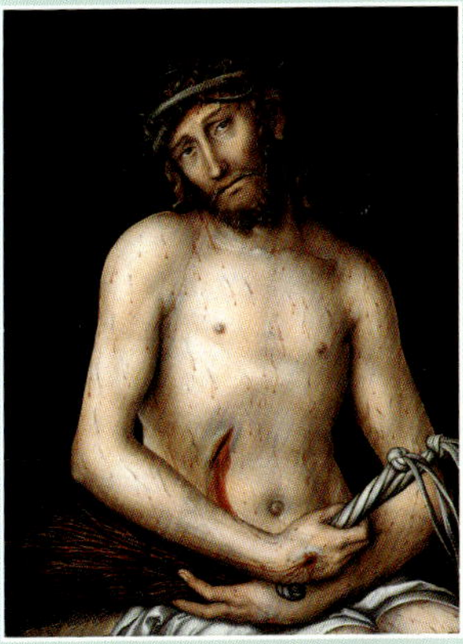

Ground Floor

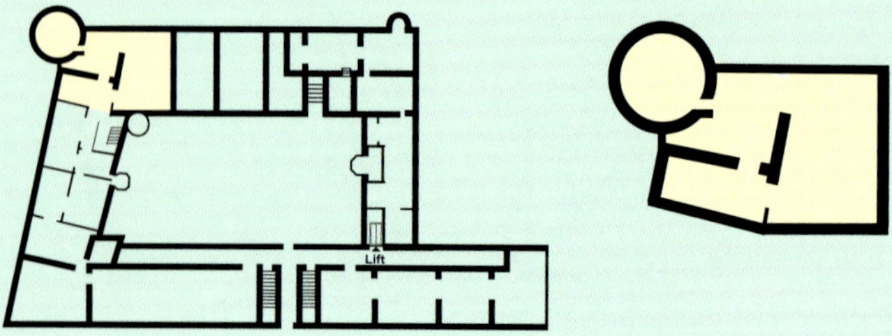

The **model** shows Gottorf as a Baroque residence with the Baroque-style Neuwerk Garden. The giant Gottorf Globe, which had a custom-built house, was famous far and wide. A slide presentation tells the history of Gottorf, from a ducal palace to the headquarters of the State Museums of Schleswig-Holstein. Sculptures preserved from the former Baroque garden, including fragments of the monumental Hercules group, are exhibited in the former kitchen of the palace. The Portrait Gallery and the Armory are further testimonies to the history of the duchy.

First Floor

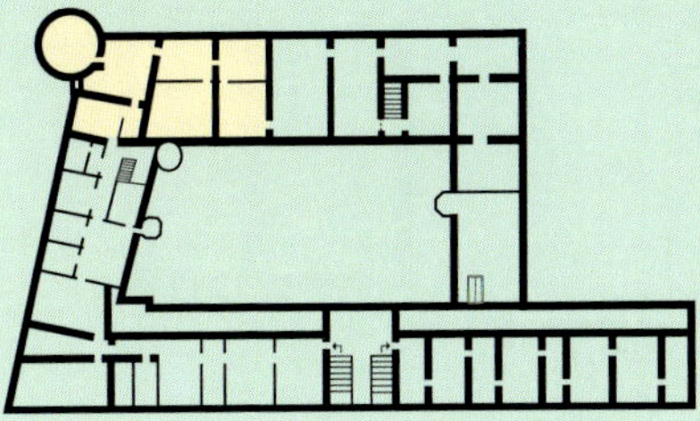

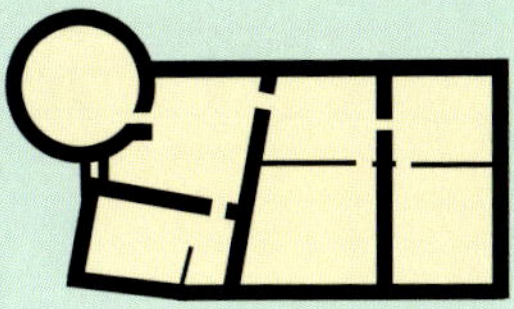

On the first floor the tour leads through a series of rooms with seventeenth-century stuccowork that is part of the original **Baroque decoration** of the palace. These rooms provide an impression of the former splendor of the residence and display works by Netherlandish and north German masters, sculptures and precious furniture. Treasures of Baroque art in ivory, serpentine, glass, gold and silver suggest the sumptuousness of the collections of the former Gottorf *Kunstkammer* (Cabinet of Curiosities).

First Floor

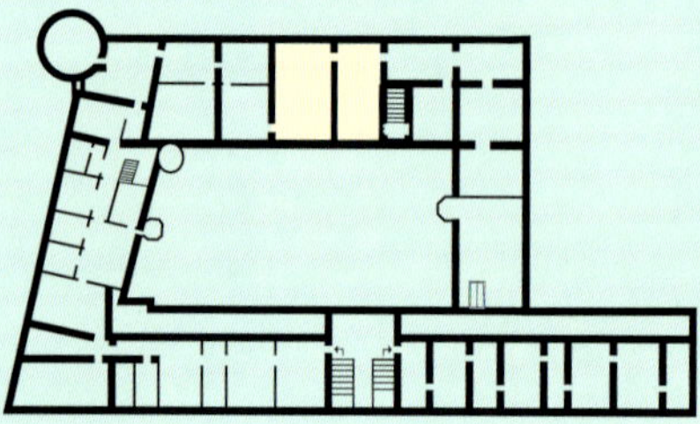

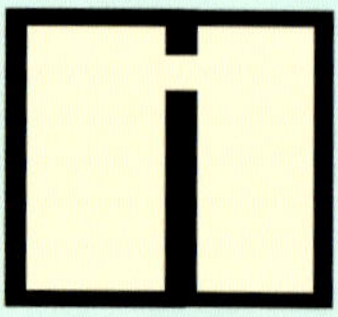

The best-preserved room in the palace is the **chapel**, dating from the 1590s. As its function never changed, it has survived in its entirety. In the early seventeenth century Duke John Adolf had a private oratory, also known as the "oven room," built with a representative, ornamental facade that looks down on to the chapel hall (see also illus. p. 106). The interior recalls an intimate room decorated with exquisite intarsia. Dating from the same period as the chapel is the Deer Hall (Hirschsaal), a Renaissance banqueting hall with life-size deer in stucco against a painted background of picturesque landscapes. Black-and-white frescoes adorn the vaulting.

First Floor

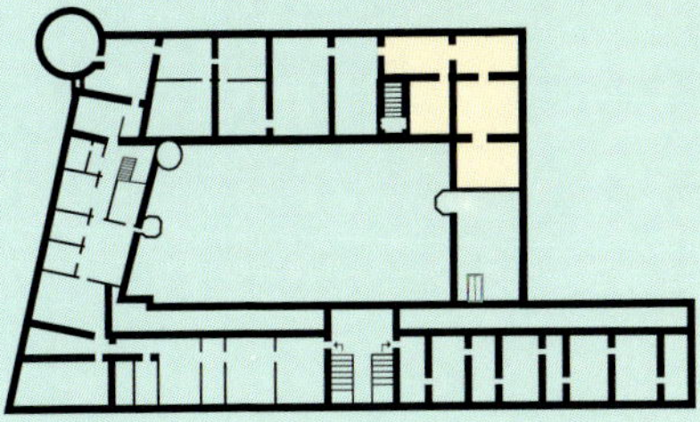

Since the Springer family bequest was made the Department of **High Baroque** and **Rococo** art has contained one of the largest collections of northern European faiences. Among its highlights are the elaborately painted tea tables. Along with the rest of the furniture, they demonstrate the elegant taste of the period, especially in the use of precious materials. The White Room with its white-and-gold Rococo paneling is from Plön Palace.

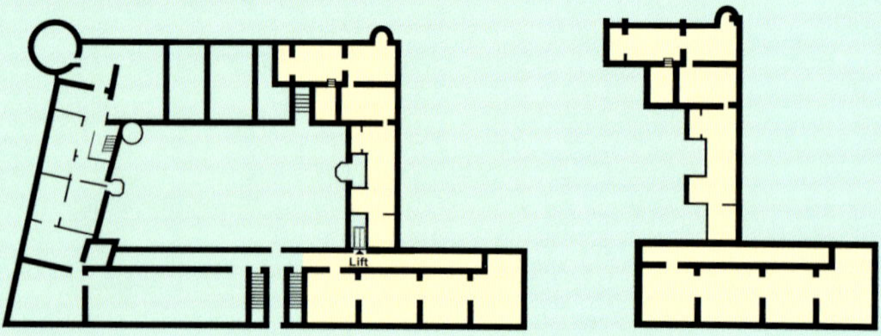

The exquisite **neoclassical furnishings** of the Emkendorf manor house, the property of Friedrich and Julia von Reventlow, including two suites of seat-furniture from Paris and Angelika Kauffmann's portrait of Julia von Reventlow, reflect the importance of the house and its residents.

The **Biedermeier** collection shows the bourgeois taste in home decor that marked the beginning of a whole new style of furniture design.

Works by major representatives of the Golden Age of Danish painting and by German realist painters can be found in the Gallery of the Nineteenth Century.

First Floor

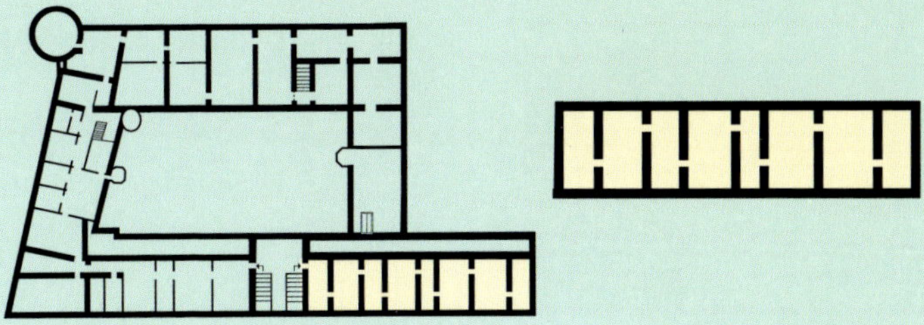

The combination of furnishings, painting, sculpture and arts and crafts in a synthesis of the arts is characteristic for **Art Nouveau** (called Jugendstil in the German-speaking world). Works based on designs by Peter Behrens, Josef Hoffmann, Henry van de Velde and Hans Christiansen demonstrate the degree to which this international, *fin de siècle* style extended to articles of everyday life, ranging from rugs and tableware to cutlery and mass-produced objects.

First Floor

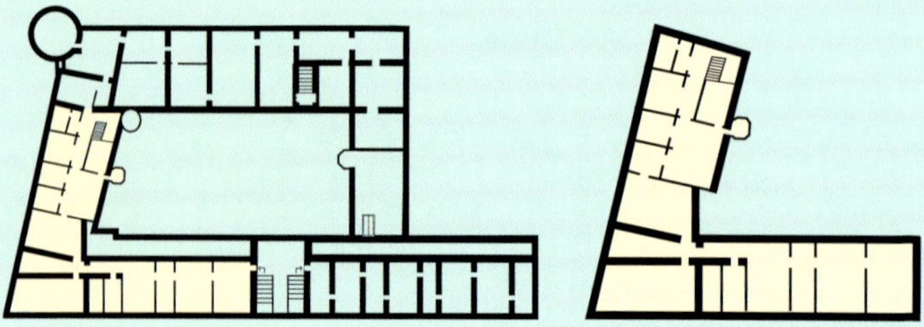

Several well-preserved **farmhouse rooms**, known as "Döns," are the central focus of the **Folk Art Department**, which is arranged according to the regions of Schleswig-Holstein.
Also on display are faience dishes, mainly from Kellinghusen, rustic furniture and traditional peasant costumes and jewelry. A separate section covers the area's seafaring past. Besides captains' pictures, it includes nautical instruments and souvenirs from past centuries.

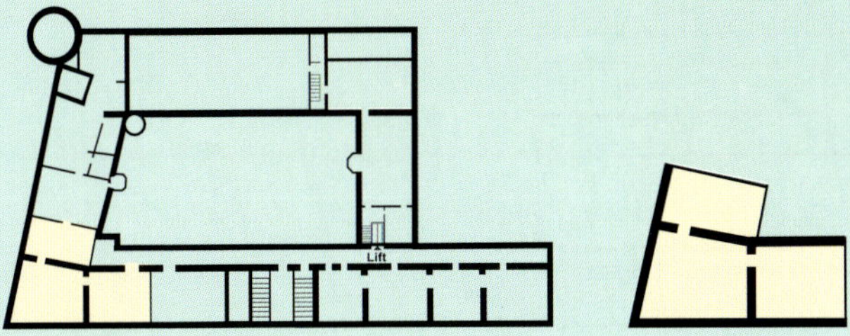

The living conditions of mankind from 120,000 to about 5000 B.C. come alive in the archaeological exhibition "**Stone-Age Hunters.**" The oldest stone tools were fashioned by the Neanderthals. Numerous finds provide information on the lives of the hunters and gatherers who lived in the tundra, near lakes and on the edges of forests. The exhibition entitled "From Hunters to Farmers" is devoted to a period of radical change, showing the earliest evidence in Schleswig-Holstein of keeping domestic animals, cultivating grain and making clay vessels.

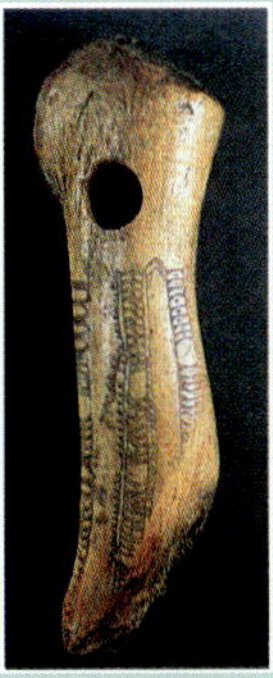

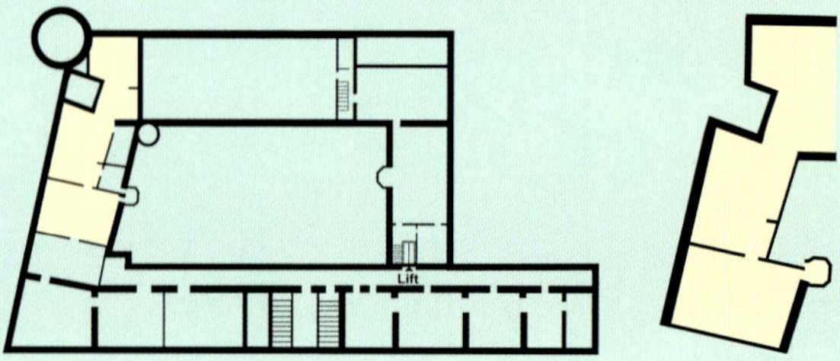

Ethnological exhibits bearing witness to the world of Stone-Age reindeer hunters are juxtaposed with those of modern reindeer breeders. Archaeological finds become easier to understand with the help of ethnological parallels from the Sami of northern Scandinavia, who live on hunting, fishing and their reindeer herds.

The ethnographic collections of Kiel University were handed over to the Archaeological Museum of the state of Schleswig-Holstein in 1995.

The workshop exhibition entitled "The World of the *Samurai*" shows the armor of the Japanese military caste, whose fascination lies in its fine craftsmanship, aesthetics and highly functional design.

Second Floor

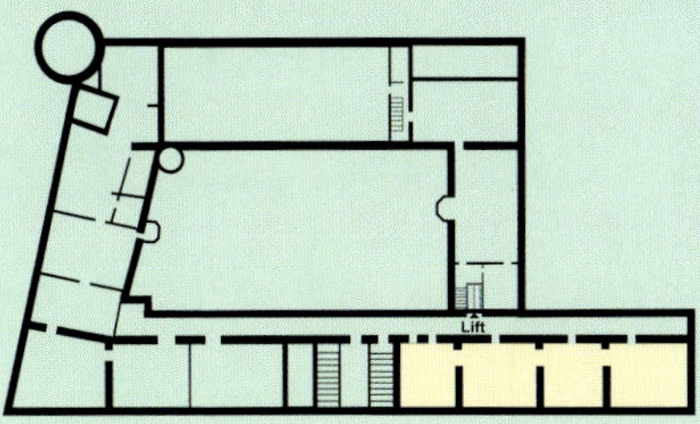

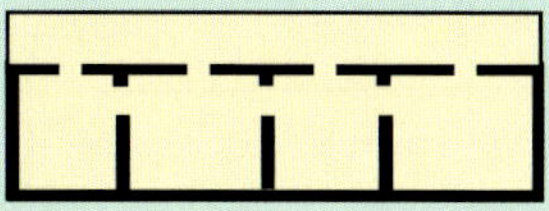

In this museum the Middle Ages are represented in two ways: in works of art, mainly ecclesiastical, and in archaeological finds. They document all areas of everyday life in the Middle Ages, providing interesting points of comparison for visitors. The thematic sections **Village, Castle, Church and Town** show groups of finds from the world of peasants and the aristocracy, the world of the devout and the clergy, and the world of the bourgeoisie. Commerce, crafts and trades, housing, clothing and food are only a few of the many subjects touched upon by the displays.

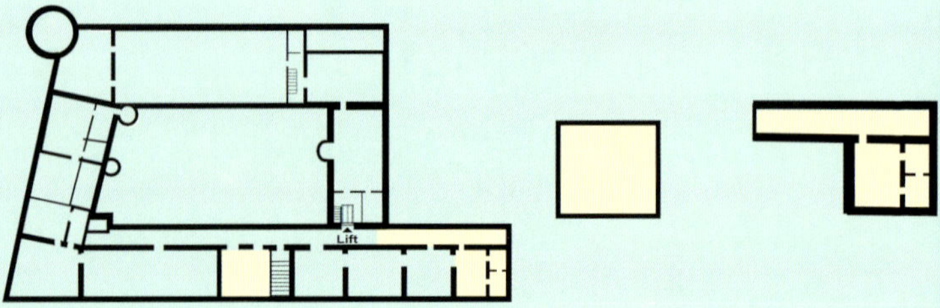

The ethnographic section "**Ethiopia** on the Eve of Revolution" includes the everyday utensils of the country's rural and urban population, which were made using traditional techniques before the overthrow of the monarchy, in 1974. A special focus is on over two hundred crosses, both pendant and hand-held types, with their wide variety of forms.
The "Holism as Objective" exhibition of the Guldager Foundation features numerous precious ethnographic objects from West Africa as well as paintings by the donor and documentation of his scientific work.

Third Floor

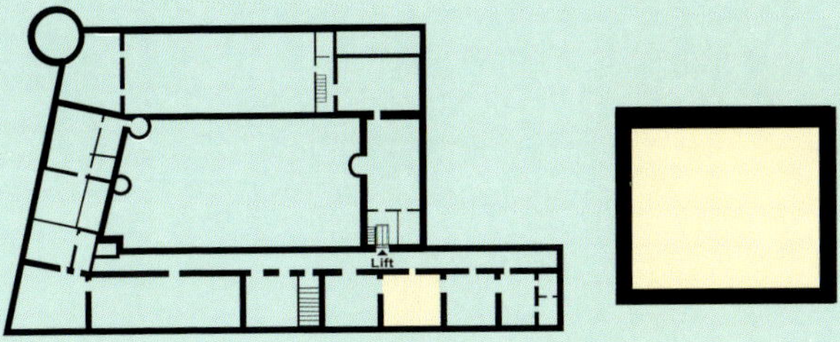

The most famous exhibits in the "Life in the **Iron Age**" section are the bog corpses. The "Windeby Girl" serves as an example to document the academic dispute on the interpretation of the find: human sacrifice, executed adulteress or the burial of a starved child? The 30,000 finds from urn graves are used to address aspects of social history, e.g., the roles of men and women, the age structure of the population, concepts of the afterlife and the development of social structures. Accounts of the Roman historian Tacitus are compared to the finds and their archaeological interpretations.

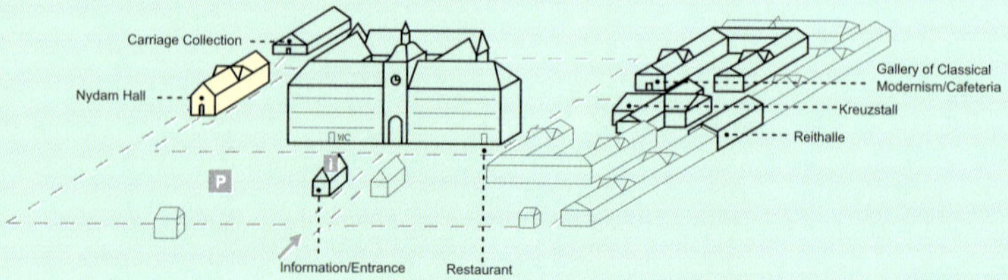

The over 1,900 objects exhibited in "Nydam and Thorsberg: Sacrificial Offerings of the Iron Age" document a dramatic episode in the history of Schleswig-Holstein. Found on the moors, they consist of war booty sacrificed by the victors of long-fought battles. The focus of interest is the **Nydam Boat**. Built about A.D. 320, some 75 feet long, 7 feet 6 inches wide and with space for a crew of about forty-five people, it is the largest oceangoing rowboat of the north known today. Military equipment and harnesses, as well as everyday furnishings and clothing, give us a vivid glimpse into the life of the Germanic peoples of the north.

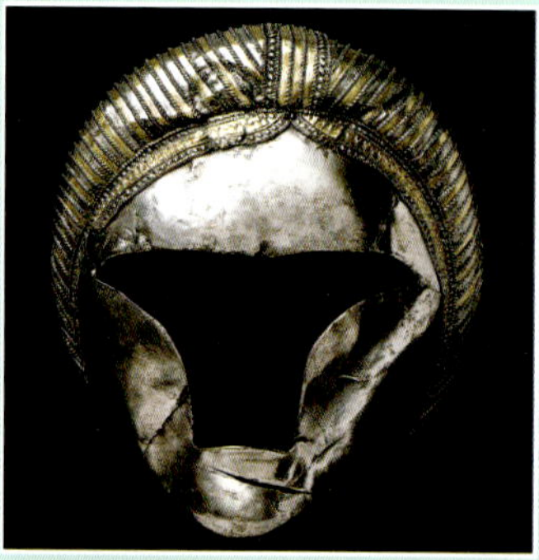

The Annexes

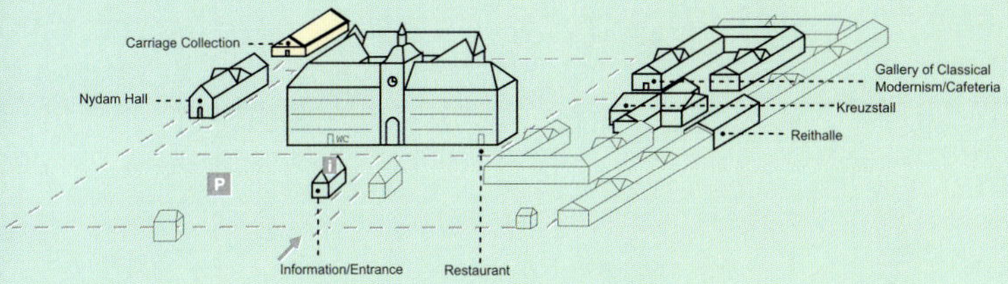

"The Life of Travel: The Journey of Life" is an exhibition that creates a vivid picture of **travel** in the nineteenth century with vehicles from estates and manor houses and of public transportation. Two large-scale display cases contain travel accessories, from beauty case to travel bathtub, portable bed to picnic set.

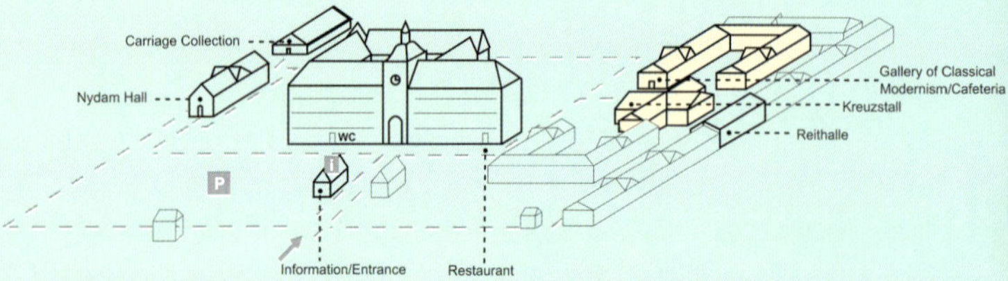

Twentieth-century painting, arts and crafts and design are shown on three floors in the Kreuzstall, a former stable.
Another large exhibition of twentieth-century art, ranging from classical modernism to the latest artistic developments, can be seen in the building next door, which houses, among other things, the Rolf Horn Foundation. Special emphasis is placed on the work of the northern German Expressionists Christian Rohlfs, Emil Nolde and Ernst Barlach. Moreover the studio of Hans Wimmer affords a good insight into the work of the sculptor.

Archaeology

From Hand Ax to Bow and Arrow: Stone-Age Hunters

The earliest archaeological finds in Schleswig-Holstein come from the vicinity of Drelsdorf, Nordfriesland county. They date back some 120,000 years, but do not seem to point to full-blown human settlement. The simple stone hand ax and several typical scraping tools were discovered at the former edge of an Ice Age glacier. Evidence was also found that a lake existed between two glacial periods, on whose shores the makers of the tools, a group of Neanderthals, spent some time. Nothing else about their living conditions could be surmised.

But from other sites, we do know that these people formed groups of experienced big-game hunters. The great significance of this discovery lies in the fact that their artifacts represent the oldest secured finds in Scandinavia. That is, these people might be called an advance guard in the early settlement of the northern European regions, and there is good reason to think more finds relating to them will be made.

From a brief, warmer period during the last glacial period, about 80,000 years ago, traces of human life have been found in a gravel pit near Schalkholz, in Dithmarschen. Yet in this case, too, the evidence is extremely scanty, nothing more than a suggestion that in this period, Schleswig-Holstein was still a Neanderthal hunting and foraging area. After that, evidence of human life here breaks off, and does not resume until the end of the later glacial period, about 14,000 years ago. A few decades ago, excavations in the Ahrensburg Tunnel Valley northeast of Hamburg unearthed sensational finds: organic traces of animals, albeit of different species than one would have hoped had survived in this fine state of preservation at the two earliest Schleswig-Holstein sites. Hundreds of reindeer antlers and bones, some still pierced with fragments of stone arrow points, permitted the reconstruction of changing hunting methods, from one-man chases to large-scale drives and bringing

Middle Paleolithic ***hand ax,*** *ca. 120,000 B.C.*

Reconstruction of a reindeer hunter's tent

down animals by forcing them into the water. One of the more recent strata even produced pine arrow shafts with still mounted stemmed points. As finds made in the excavations near Poggenwisch appear to indicate, reindeer hunters of the late Iron Age were tent-dwellers.

Tests on pollen found in peat strata tell us about climate changes at the end of the Ice Age. The glacial layers are interrupted by a deposit that goes back to a temporary warming, during which reindeer vanished and tundra gave way to the first coniferous woods, roamed by elk and beaver. Finds along the northern margin of then-populated Europe reflect the reactions of Ice Age hunters to slight changes in the natural environment, in terms of hunting methods, weapons and the size of hunting groups. About 11,000 years ago, the great northern European inland glacier receded to the far north of Scandinavia,

and the climate rapidly grew warmer. Evidence of temperature increases has been found by testing local fossilized insects and analyzing ice drill cores from Greenland.

The first trees began to spread—birches, pines and hazel bushes, followed by species of the typical mixed oak forest: oaks, elms and lindens. The initially sparse woods soon proliferated into dense primeval forests. Regional climate changes continued to occur. The vast herds of reindeer had migrated north, to be replaced by non-migrating species from the south—aurochs, red deer, roe deer and wild boars. The countryside was punctuated by thousands of lakes and ponds rich in fish, relics of the scouring force of glaciers. This was the habitat of Mesolithic man, and the source of the first discovered traces indicating how *homo sapiens sapiens* dealt with interglacial climate conditions.

Nourishment came from whatever could be brought down with a bow and arrow. Early man also fished with harpoons, wicker weirs and nets, and gathered berries and herbs. A staple of their diet was hazelnuts, rich in calories and capable of long storage, found in hazel groves in the open woods of the post-glacial period.

For years now, excavations have been undertaken in one of the settlements in these nomadic hunters' territories, in the Duvenseer Moor. Strictly speaking, this was not a settlement at all but a group of temporary camps on a lakeshore and small islands, where hazelnuts harvested in autumn were roasted—a preservation process that prevented the formation of toxic mold. People sat around the fire, protected from the cold, damp ground by birchbark mats, predecessors of today's insulating mats. Groups of hunter-gatherers lived along lakes and rivers; a pinewood paddle bears witness to their semi-aquatic way of life. Lumps of birch pitch with tooth impressions

***Reindeer hunters' harpoons** found at Stellmoor near Ahrensburg (Stormarn county), ca. 8300 B.C.*

would suggest dental care with the aid of primitive chewing gum. The finds made in these camps provide a picture of human life and living conditions 10,000 years ago. They include elaborate and very precisely datable remnants of hunting weapons that reflect certain waves of development, which were by no means strictly functional but must also have been culturally determined.

The world of the hunters and gatherers came to an end in this region about 6,000 years ago. After beginning to spread from the Near East five millennia earlier, the Neolithic economy reached the northern boundaries of the inhabited world, bringing modified plants—especially cereals—and domesticated cattle and pigs. The Stone Age with its agrarian economy, forerunner of modern civilization, had begun. Yet the character of civilization had been determined by three million years of the hunting life. One wonders whether the modern world has truly come to terms with its genetic hunting heritage. *KB*

The Boat from Nydam Moor and a Forgotten War: Nydam Hall

A huge boat built of oak, nearly 76 feet long and a good eight tons heavy, blackened by centuries of lying deep in the moor plus nineteenth-century conservation measures, is a veritable veteran of early European history. This is not a Viking ship, as excited viewers tend to believe, for it is half a millennium older than any Viking ship. The boat that has found its last harbor in the converted Gottorf cavalry drill hall is the earliest known oceangoing vessel in northern Europe, the oldest and largest surviving ship built by a Germanic tribe. While most Viking ships had to be largely reconstructed, this ancient veteran was discovered in 70 percent perfect condition.

As studies of the wood growth rings show, the ship's keel must have been laid about A.D. 320. This was the period preceding the great migration of peoples, when caesars still ruled in Rome, Christianity began to spread and the remote Baltic region began to be settled by Germanic tribes, about whom we know little more than a handful of names—Angles, Jutes, Suions. The primitive nature of the ship's construction corresponds to its early date.

From giant oaks whose trunks grew straight and strong about fifty feet high, fourteen planks were hewn with axes, fitted together into sides with the aid of iron rivets and affixed to the keel plank. Inside each plank, hand-sized projections with holes, were left standing at regular intervals. These were the attachment points for the ship's timbers, or "ribs." Ballast and load were covered by a wooden deck, where the rowers' feet rested—the ship was propelled forward by oarsmen, for there is no sign that it had a mast or sail. The oars rested

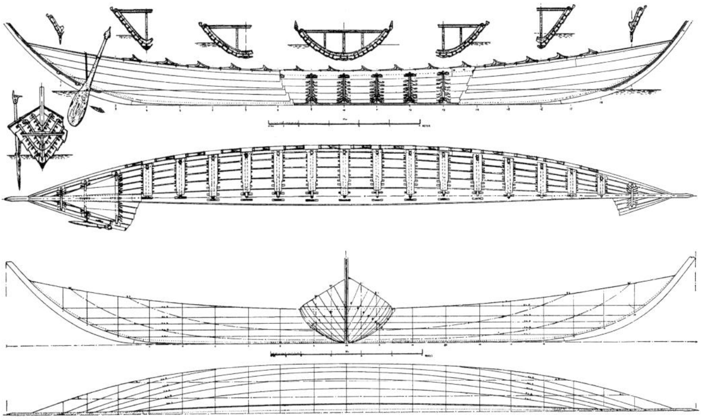

The Nydam Boat, a Germanic warship, reconstruction by Shetelig and Johannesson

The Nydam Boat, Baltic region, ca. A.D. 320, oak, 39 ⅜ x 905 ½ x 137 ¾ in., weight: approx. 8 tons

in hook-shaped locks of alder or poplar wood. These soft-wood pivots were lashed to the gunwale and could be easily replaced when they had been worn down by the hard oak oars.

Thirty men could sit on the fifteen thwarts, and one presumably operated the great rudder at the stern; the crew may have consisted of as many as forty-five. The vessel's purpose was evidently use in war. With its narrow hull and identical, sharp bow and stern posts, it was likely capable of high speeds—in either direction, if need be. This adapted it perfectly to maneuvering in the fjords, bays and estuaries along the Baltic coasts. The ship was not designed to transport large amounts of cargo but to carry warriors, their weapons and

—assuming success—their booty. But how did it come to rest in the moor? And what is the story behind its discovery?

Excavations carried out around the middle of the nineteenth century in Nydam Moor, opposite Alsen Island in present-day Denmark, brought not only the ship to light but remnants of two further boats (which have not survived) and far more than one thousand weapons. One of these is in especially good condition: a double-edged iron sword from the fourth century A.D., nearly 3 feet long and weighing approximately 1 pound 12 ounces. The tang originally bore a hilt of organic material, which decayed in ancient times. The thin lines parallel to the edges of the blade indicate its method of manufacture. Thin bands of high- and low-carbon iron were forged into a flat bar, to which the two cutting edges were attached. Carbon content makes iron hard, but also brittle, while soft, low-carbon iron is tough and flexible, which prevents breakage. Their combination results in a blade that has the properties of steel, whose manufacture in modern quality was then still unknown. Its complicated forging technique, requiring high crafting skills, was prevalent in the Roman Empire, and was known as damascene.

In addition to the damascene markings, the blade evinces signs of damage—two dents and several notches—that probably resulted from its use. One can imagine the small vertical notches toward the point having been made when the sword crossed that of a defender, and the long, diagonal incisions near the handle resulting from parrying an enemy's blows. The owner of this sword struck at least eleven times, and had to ward off at least two close attacks. Over 1,600 years lie between us and these events. The warriors have long fallen to dust, their names are unknown, the cause of their altercation obscure. Yet the traces on this weapon vividly evoke a dramatic confrontation that likely cost a human life; and beyond this, they shed light on a whole chain of historically significant events whose explanation must rely on archaeologists' expertise.

In fact, the present sword is only one of more than one hundred similar ones found together with the ship. Also uncovered were nearly 400 lances and 350 spears, about 70 shields, about 40 bows and as many axes, and over 200 arrows—arms for over 500 men, now preserved at Gottorf and a selection of which is on display. Standardized types of weapon and nearly identical numbers would indicate that they were used by a large body of troops, well organized along Roman lines.

The weapons' excellent state of preservation permits many conclusions to be drawn about methods of fabrication. The birch pitch used to affix feathers to the arrow shafts, for instance, still contains remnants of the swan and eagle feathers that were frequently employed. Signs of varying degrees of artisanal skill are also evident. One arrow was the work of a perfectionist, who additionally secured the feathers with 64 winds of thread along nearly 4 inches of shaft; another was made by a lazy fellow who thought 16 winds sufficient. And the latter apparently got literally stuck to his work, because his fingers raised lumps in the pitch and the feathers ended up crooked. Signs of left-handed craftsmen can be seen, or of unpracticed ones who cut the notch for the bowstring with the grain instead of across it. In short, we find traces of human individuality and failings that seem to indicate that rather than stemming from professional industry, these arrows were made by the more or less dexterous bowmen themselves. Many of the other weapons attest to a final battle—notches left by blows on lances, bent hooks on spearheads or incisions in plank shields evoke a resounding clash between teeming war parties.

Other signs of damage are evidently not the result of battle. Many of the swords were thrown in a fire and purposely bent. The metal hand-protector on many a shield was repeatedly pierced from inside by a spear or completely smashed with an ax. The explanation for such damage is found in Roman sources—it was an ancient Germanic custom, after a successful battle, to sacrifice captured weapons in thanks to a helpful god by destroying and sinking them. The Nydam ship and weapons, in other words, apparently represent war booty from extensive, as yet only archaeologically recorded battles that shook the western Baltic region on the eve of the Anglo-Saxon migration—and that perhaps even contributed in part to this historical process. *MG*

Life in the Iron Age: The "Windeby Girl"

Among the eras of primeval and early history, the Iron Age—the millennium from 500 B.C. to A.D. 500—plays a special role in Schleswig-Holstein. Iron is only one of the aspects that make this era so fascinating. At its beginning, this material was imported into the region and forged into weapons and implements; by its end, iron was being locally mined and processed.

Even more important are the various sources that allow us to paint a detailed picture of human life at this period. This is not possible for any other era in Schleswig-Holstein's early history.

Rich evidence of Iron Age settlement has been found in man-made mounds on the west coast of the state that contain remnants of long houses. The religious practices of this early people are reflected in extraordinary finds made in the moors, evidence of sacrifices to the gods ranging from single clay pots containing humble foods, to arsenals for an entire army. The acidic water of the moors has preserved materials that would rapidly decay in normal soils: wooden boats, bows and arrows, even the skin and hair of human beings and animals—that is, wool and leather clothing such as cloaks, shirts, trousers, belts and shoes, and in special cases even human bodies, known as bog corpses. As a rule, however, the dead were cremated in that period and buried in urns.

While only one to two thousand graves from other eras have been discovered, the Iron Age with its huge urn burial grounds has yielded the graves of approximately 30,000 people in Schleswig-Holstein alone. Owing to cremation on funeral pyres, the bones were calcinated and rendered impervious to plants and microorganisms. This ensured the survival of skeletal remains, even some of tiny infants, down to this day. The abundance of material permits conclusions to be drawn about age,

The "Windeby Girl"

sex and illnesses, thus providing unique clues as to the demographic and—in connection with burial goods—sociohistorical conditions of the period. Records in the concurrently emerging runic script convey the earliest proper names, but also information about magical ideas and rites.

But most importantly, the light of Mediterranean historiography was now shed on this ancient realm between the North and Baltic Seas. Roman chronicles recorded the names of individual tribes and their leaders, reported on their activities, battles and migrations, and described them as "Germanic" peoples, who began to exert a manifest influence on the course of European history. More on this topic can be found in the exhibition "Life in the Iron Age."

The "Windeby Girl," a bog corpse who has since found her way into schoolbooks, films, detective stories and songs worldwide and draws countless visitors to Gottorf Palace, was discovered near Windeby Estate outside Eckernförde.

The thirteen- or fourteen-year-old girl lies on her right side, and seems to have been buried unclothed. Parts of her body are covered with peat; her eyes are concealed by a narrow band. Almost two thousand years separate our lives from hers. We cannot help but

wonder what thoughts and emotions moved this girl. How many of them would be familiar to us, and how many were bound up with a world that has inexorably disintegrated to dust? And—do her features reveal a glimmer of knowledge of those things experienced only in the hour of death, a test we all face sooner or later? Many visitors find themselves deeply moved by the sight of this girl.

For all its cultural and historical interest, it is a dead person first and foremost. Not merely a skeleton but a body conserved by humic acid. It is vaguely eerie, with a touch of the macabre. Lying there in the showcase, the girl is not unattractive. Her firm bare thighs, and an attitude suggesting adolescent yearnings, might well seem alluring, were it not for the brown, leathery skin, the protruding ribs and the grisly fate this girl apparently suffered in the moor. This, I am afraid, is exactly what many find so tantalizing.

The conventional scientific interpretation has contributed not a little to this impression. Various explanations have been given for the phenomenon of bog corpses, bodies dating to the centuries around the birth of Christ and frequently found in the regions bordering the North Sea. Some believe they represent human sacrifices. As numbers of offerings found in such places indicate, the moors were clearly thought of as sacred sites. In the ninth chapter of his ethnographic account *Germania*, the Roman historian Tacitus confirms the existence of such sacrificial customs in the first century A.D. On the other hand, in chapter twelve he describes the Germanic custom of punishing "immoral" or "battle-shy" persons by drowning them in a moor. Many of the bog corpses, including the three male ones in our exhibition, attest to such violence—decapitation, smashed skulls, knife wounds in the heart.

Such injuries were not found in the case of the Windeby Girl. This led researchers to turn to chapter nineteen of *Germania*, where Tacitus tells how cuckolded husbands would whip their unfaithful wives through the village, naked, their heads shorn.... The right side of the Windeby Girl's head has short hair, and the left is shorn. Apart from the blindfold and a short cowhide cape, no further apparel has survived. Might she have been executed for adultery? Her raised right hand performs the gesture known as the fig, with thumb thrust between index and middle finger—a commonly known obscene gesture with sexual connotations. Several feet from the site where the girl was found, a male body was discovered in the moor, a hazel switch noose around his neck—the girl's seducer? The suspicion of a cruelly avenged sin grew increasingly probable. Are these two corpses in fact silent witnesses to an erotic drama that played itself out two thousand years ago?

As a thorough reinvestigation subsequently revealed, the girl had been buried with four clay vessels in a pit lined with heather. Previously unavailable personal photographs, taken by a witness to the excavation, clearly showed that her hand was not originally closed into a fist with protruding thumb, nor was the right arm extended. The dead girl lay on her right side in a sleeping position, covered—perhaps lovingly—with cotton-grass. The find corresponded in detail with contemporaneous earth burials on the Jutland peninsula.

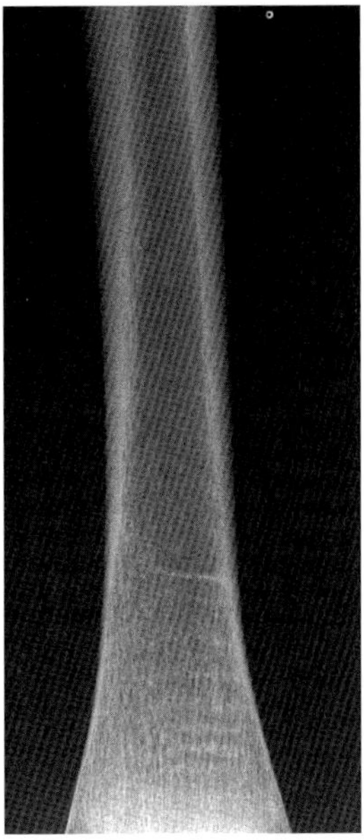

X-ray. The eleven so-called growth lines on the shin of the "Windeby Girl" attest to repeated periods of famine

Other considerations shed further doubt on the sexual drama hypothesis. Tacitus makes no mention of the execution of unfaithful wives (who "later cannot find a new husband"), nor was the girl naked when she was buried. Though humic acid has preserved the cowhide cape, it can decompose plant textiles, so the body may originally have been clad, say, in linen underclothing. Tacitus, like Julius Caesar before him, reports that the Germans married at a very late age, as a rule not before their twentieth year, and archaeological investigations appear to confirm this. So at the worst, the girl could have been the victim of an adulterer much her elder. Yet her blindfolded eyes and one-sidedly shorn hair could be traced back to any number of causes. Despite a millennium of Christian education, many popular beliefs survived, including the removal of hair from sick or deceased persons for magical reasons. Also, and strikingly, only that part of the head is shorn which had to be scraped free with a trowel before reaching the torso.

The question as to the cause of the girl's death, finally, can be answered without resorting to imagined scenarios. An X-ray of the tibia shows eleven growth lines, which occur only when growth temporarily stagnates due to malnutrition or the stress of a serious illness. The regular spacing of these lines suggests repeated periods of famine in late winter—a fate this girl surely shared with others in a community that was compelled to bury about half of their children prematurely. The formation of a twelfth line may have been forestalled by death.

All in all, one suspects that the association of this bog corpse with sex and crime, aided and abetted by science, has influenced its general interpretation. Still, much remains unexplained, such as the male corpse with the noose around its neck, and the unusual burial of the girl in the moor. The solution to this riddle remains open to speculation, as does the nature of the world in which the girl lived.

Imagination is aided by a look at the thousands of "normal" graves that can help us reconstruct everyday life in that period. General life expectancy was less than thirty years; arthritis, vertebral and dental diseases were a daily fact of life; nor was cancer unknown. Men and women reached an average height of 5 feet 8 inches and 5 feet 2 inches, respectively. If a man was lucky enough to survive to the venerable age of forty or older, he was honored by placing weapons, alcoholic beverages, luxury and cosmetic articles in his grave. In contrast, women of whatever age were generally sent to the afterworld wearing plain costumes and accompanied by their handiwork. A few rich graves containing Roman-style goods contrast with hundreds of humble burials.

Neither the Windeby Girl nor the women of her era could have dreamed of the advancements that would be made by their sex in centuries to come.

MG

Wikinger Museum Haithabu: Window on an Early Medieval Town

"Bucking stallion on the salty paths of the salmon"—the scaldic verses of ancient Scandinavian poets evoke Viking ships in richly facetted imagery, pointing to their great significance for the medieval world. A ship of this type is the focus of the presentation at the Wikinger Museum Haithabu (Viking Museum Haithabu). This extraordinary find, discovered by a deep-sea diver in 1953, was raised in 1979 during a spectacular archaeological investigation at Hadde-

The boat hall and museum's shipyard

by Noor. Its conserved wooden parts were reassembled into a section of the foreship by a boatbuilder.

In terms of the shipbuilding art, the find is special in many respects. At an original length of nearly 100 feet and a maximum width of approximately 8 feet 10 inches, the ship was of an unusually slender type. The hull has extremely thin planking, and every structural detail was designed for strength and lightness. "Long and light runs well," as boatbuilders say. One marine archaeologist thinks a speed of up to 15 or 20 knots conceivable. Neither a logbook nor the ship's name or home harbor were found to shed light on the wreck. Scientific studies, however, were able to glean valuable clues from its planks: dendrochronological dating indicates that the lumber for the ship was cut around the year 982. A characteristic pollen spectrum from the caulking material suggests that the shipyard lay in the coastal area of the region.

But who commissioned the vessel? In view of the carefully planed and fitted planks, which were radially split from straight, tall trunks, it becomes obvious that very high-quality building material was employed. The fine craftsmanship reveals the hand of a master. Extremely thin planks required a "close stitching" of iron rivets,

The "Eric Stone," ca. A.D. 1000, memorial stone with runic inscription, granite, h. 95 5/8 in.

The semicircular rampart at Haithabu

which in turn implied a "fat pouch of silver" for the smith. Perhaps the ship was commissioned by a monarch? Whatever the case, this long ship is a superb example of warships of the Viking era, which were designed to take a large crew.

In early medieval northern Europe, shipping was the prime motor of advancing civilization. Oceangoing ships provided the mobility that was a precondition for the exchange of ideas and experiences. Hefty cargo vessels ensured transport capacities without which an extensive trading of goods would have been inconceivable over 1,000 years ago.

And who were the seamen who sailed such ships as traders or warriors? One of them is immortalized in an inscription on a rune stone.

Clothes pin in the form of a dragon's head, bronze, l. 6 ¼ in.

It tells us of a man by the name of Eric: "… he was steersman—a worthy warrior." Back then, steering a ship meant heading the crew, like a captain. And owning one lent high social status to the close-knit group of seafarers.

Traders sailed from harbor to harbor to participate in the lively exchange of goods that took place there. Haithabu, located on a bay in the Schlei, was one such harbor town. Founded in 808 at this geographically favorable site between the North and Baltic Seas by King Godefrid of Denmark, it expanded in the ninth and tenth centuries into a prosperous center of trade and craftsmanship.

Under royal protection, local artisans made products both for the local community and for export abroad. One of Haithabu's trade contacts was Novgorod, Russia, where glass beads were shipped. In exchange, bones and antlers, bars of bronze and lead, pieces of amber and jet, were brought here as raw materials and worked into combs and needles, jewelry, amulets and tokens for games. Exquisite filigree gold jewelry was fabricated in workshops and displayed in the hope of attracting a buyer.

People from far and wide came to Haithabu on trading ships. Their origins and social standing were reflected in their gravesites. The most elaborate yet found was located in a mound, concealed by an upturned ship's hull. Rich accoutrements for the life after death pointed to a royal burial. On his way to the beyond, the deceased man was accompanied not only by two of his retinue but by his horses as well. The ship was a symbol of status and a vessel well suited for the journey to Valhalla, where warriors were welcomed at Odin's table.

Ships also brought the new faith to the Nordic realm. Christian missionaries came by sea to Haithabu, where they founded its first church around the year 850. The gradual conversion of the populace is reflected in the coexistence of relics of heathen and Christian symbolism. Hammer-shaped amulets attest to the worship of the god of thunder, Thor, while crucifixes document the increasing influence of the Christian church.

Terslev fibula, 10th century A.D., brooch, gold, diam. 1 ¼ in.

Haithabu—a world in transition and "a very large city at the extreme end of the world sea," noted the Arabian traveler At Tartushi, who came here from the Califate of Cordoba in 965. Haithabu was truly a large town for the period. About 1,000 people lived within its semicircular rampart. It must have been a lively place, noisy, colorful and teeming with harbor life. Today, peace pervades the site, which is now used as grazing land.

But with a little imagination, we can picture in our mind's eye the contours of the old town rising from the meadows, where except for the rampart, nothing remains to recall its heyday. "Of these cities will remain that which passed through them, the wind!" (Bertolt Brecht) *UD*

Village—Castle—Church—Town: Schleswig and Holstein in the Middle Ages

In 1976, excavations were conducted in considerably disturbed twelfth- and thirteenth-century settlement strata in Schleswig's Old Town near the shores of the Schlei. One of the objects brought to light was the present gold fibula, or brooch. Its openwork, convex middle section and its eight pearl-wire drums forming the edge bear glass-paste inlays of various colors, a few of which are missing. Based on its stylistic traits, the piece can be dated to the second quarter of the eleventh century, and attributed to a workshop that supplied the Salian imperial dynasty. This is underscored by close parallels with the goldsmith technique of the imperial crown and the cross of Emperor Conrad II (ca. 1030). Typical ornamental elements suggest that the goldsmith originated from the Mediterranean region. A number of comparable pieces are known from Minden, Mainz and other locations. This precious piece of jewelry surely once belonged to a wealthy and high-ranking lady.

***Fibula**, ca. 1030, gold, glass paste, diam. 1 ⅜ in., found in Schleswig*

Whether it was purchased from a dealer or directly from the goldsmith, or was perhaps even a gift from the emperor, remains just as much a matter of speculation as the circumstances that brought it to the site where it was found, the corner of a house in the harbor district of Schleswig. Yet though its path remains obscure, the find does link the city with the most eminent circles in the German Empire, its leading aristocratic families and imperial court. One is tempted to imagine the clasp in connection with a dynastic wedding: In autumn 1042, Wulfhild, sister of King Magnus I Olafsson of Denmark and Norway, was given in marriage to Ordulf, son of Duke Bernhard II of Saxony, by the Archbishop of Bremen, Bezelin Alebrand. Could the piece have been stately jewelry presented at a marriage of state? Whatever the case, it is an archaeological rule that such valuable finds are rare exceptions.

Nor have great numbers survived even of articles that were mass-produced in the Middle Ages, such as pilgrims' emblems. Our museum contains a considerable collection, however. One is a badge from the pilgrimage town of Notre-Dame de Rocamadour, found in excavations in Schleswig. The field of the pointed oval in seal form with six loops bears a depiction of the Virgin enthroned, with a low, three-pointed crown and halo. In her right hand is a scepter with a many-branched blossom. The infant Jesus, seated frontally on her knee and clad in a long gown, has the pose and proportions of a young adult. His hand, raised in blessing or to speak, points to his mother. The inscription in majuscules reads: "+ SIGILLUM : BEATEMARIE : DEROCAMADOR."

***Pilgrims' badge** from Notre-Dame de Rocamadour, France, 13th century, lead-pewter alloy, 2 7/8 x 2 1/4 in., found in Schleswig*

Pilgrims' badges were devotional items that were distributed by the thousands at sacred sites. At St. Mary's Shrine in Einsiedeln, for instance, about 130,000 of them were passed out during fourteen days in September of the year 1466. The great majority of these emblems are flat castings in a lead-pewter alloy. The meaning, value and significance of pilgrims' badges lie on many levels. Worn on a hat or coat or attached to a walking stick, they provided protection during the pilgrim's journey, and represented a silent entreaty for alms. As contact reliquaries, they were believed to be imbued with the vital force of the saints worshiped at the place of pilgrimage. They were also associated with a range of popular beliefs and medical cures, including magical and superstitious practices.

Rocamadour, in the southern French region of Quercy, owed its rise from a local shrine of the Virgin to an international pilgrimage destination to the burgeoning of the northern Spanish cult of St. Jacob in the eleventh and twelfth centuries. Although located off the main pilgrimage route to Santiago de Compostela, Rocamadour became a focus of the great European pilgrimage movement. Between 1166 and 1172, 126 miraculous healings were recorded in its book of wonders. In the late Middle Ages, Rocamadour was renowned as a destination for pilgrimages of punishment and atonement for sins, which earned the town a correspondingly equivocal reputation.

Coffins from Schleswig cemeteries. Wooden coffins from cemetery located at the site of Schleswig's marketplace in front of the town hall, 11th–12th century, brick tomb from St. Nicholas's, 13th century

As travel documents, pilgrims' badges give an idea of the mass mobility of people during the Middle Ages. Of the hundreds of thousands of such emblems that must have been issued at Rocamadour, only about forty are known to have survived—apart from Schleswig, at Scandinavian sites such as Lund, Helsingborg and Bergen.

Medieval man looked upon life itself as a pilgrimage, in which every activity revolved around a concern for eternal redemption. The end of the earthly journey, death, with which people were continually confronted, is almost tangible in a collection of coffins at Gottorf. These came from a cemetery once located on the square (Rathausmarkt) in front of Schleswig's town hall. After the secularization, the cemetery was covered at some point by a thick layer of rich dung, sealing the coffins off from the air and preserving them. As a dendrochronological study of the wood indicates, the trees used to build them were felled between about 1080 and the beginning of the thirteenth century—making this the oldest extensively investigated cemetery in the entire country. Coffins of children and adolescents confirm the demographic data obtained from the skeletons. Infant mortality among the Schleswig population was about 29 percent, and their average life expectancy only 21.7 years.

Like living, dying in the Middle Ages was subject to a precisely defined code of conduct, a public ritual at whose end stood interment in consecrated ground. Every body was buried facing the Holy Land in the East. Even in the Christian era, graves continued to reflect both ideas of the afterlife and the social status of the deceased during their lifetimes. Burial in a coffin was a prerogative of the prosperous, and a stone sarcophagous even more so. Many a poor person could not even afford a shroud.

The medieval period is the most recent one in the state's history to be represented in archaeological finds. It followed chronologically upon the Viking era, which, owing to the great international significance of the Haithabu finds, is displayed in a separate exhibition at the Wikinger Museum Haithabu. Medieval archaeology being a relatively young discipline in this region, the objects in the Medieval Department stem largely from excavations made over the past few decades, most outstandingly those in Schleswig's Old Town. These were the source of the majority of finds on display.

The division of the Medieval Department into thematic sections of village, castle, church and town reflects the key social strata of the era—peasantry, nobility, clergy and citizenry—and in this way illustrates the principal aim of the collection, which is to convey an archaeologically documented history of the state. *CR*

Ethnology

The World of the *Samurai*: Japanese Armor at Gottorf Palace

An outstanding part of the ethnological collections is the Japanese *samurai* armor. Most of it comes from the collection of Prince Henry of Prussia (1862–1929), who, as Grand Admiral of the Fleet, had his official residence in the Kiel palace. Around the turn of the century the diplomatic missions he carried out on behalf of his brother, Emperor William II, took him to China and Japan.

From 1185 to 1868 powerful commanders-in-chief (*shoguns*) and members of the military caste (*samurai*) ruled feudal Japan. They essentially also determined the social and cultural life of the country. The ideals and codes of conduct of the military ruling class took shape under the influence of Zen Buddhism. Life's fulfillment was seen in warfare and in the unconditional dedication to one's overlord and the *shogun*. Nevertheless, life did not consist of war alone. Culture, too, played an important role.

Apart from the tea ceremony, the Nō theater is perhaps the best known form of creative expression of the military caste. Developed in the fourteenth century from the religious drama of the temple festivals, it soon lost its popular character. The stylized performance with very few gestures turned into a ceremonial production for and by the aristocracy. All parts were played by men. Masks indicated the sex, age and social position of the characters.

The beginning of the *samurai* period is the subject of a unique tapestry dating from the nineteenth century. It shows a key incident in the famous sea battle of Dannoura, fought in March 1185. The leader of the Minamoto clan, Yoshitsune, is shown in the middle of the picture performing his heroic "leap across eight boats." Tomomori, the leader of the Taira clan, stands in a boat in the right foreground with his foster brother Iga Ienaga. With the victory of the Minamoto over the Taira, the emperor and his court lost all temporal power and withdrew to their religious and ritual functions. By establishing a hereditary *shogunate*, Minamoto Yoritomo set up the military rule that was to last until 1868.

The *samurai* constituted the military basis of the *shogunate*'s power and were part of the central and provincial government administration. Their status was manifested primarily in their weapons and armor.

Japanese armor is particularly fascinating not only for its aesthetic and outstandingly functional design but also its extraordinary

Scene from the ***sea battle of Dannoura*** *(1185), 19th century, tapestry, silk embroidery, 80 7/8/83 1/4 x 66 3/4/67 5/8 in.*

Samurai ***suit of armor***, *15th–first half of 18th century, composite armor, suit of a high-ranking officer, skin, lacquer, metal, silk*

longevity. The same forms were revived, varied and re-produced time and again throughout a period of almost eight hundred years. Entire suits or parts of suits of armor could be handed down from one generation to the next.

By the beginning of the Kamakura period (1192–1338) three styles and techniques had evolved that continued to be important for the next six hundred years. *O-Yoroi*, *haramaki* and *do maru* armor differ mainly in function and in the difficulty and expense involved in their manufacture. The quality of the craftsmanship, the colors and the uniformity of the equipment as well as the heraldic badges refer to the rank and clan membership of the wearer.

O-Yoroi was the magnificent, heavy armor of the mounted aristocratic archers. The infantry wore the lighter and more simply equipped *do maru* or, from the fourteenth century on, the equally simple *haramaki*. These lighter styles worn by foot soldiers evolved into modern forms of armor in the sixteenth century.

The finest suit in the ethnological collections is Prince Henry's *daimyo* armor no. 17. It shows the wealth of subtle detail and the consummate craftsmanship that went in to fashioning matching ensembles for the leading members of the military caste.

The floral metal decoration showing the heraldic device, the ornamentation of the metal trimmings and toggles citing elements of the heraldic device, as well as the silk brocade on which the suit is mounted are characteristic of such high-quality workmanship. Moreover, the largely traditional techniques used to make it involved considerably more work than simpler armor did.

The collection serves to illustrate the typical styles of armor and other equipment of the period. Furthermore, it demonstrates the range of quality extending from the mercenary's simple equipment to the *daimyo*'s very elaborate suit. Chronologically it covers the periods from Late Muromachi to Late Edo (from the sixteenth to nineteenth century), with composite armor or at least reassembled suits predominating. The majority of the armor is relatively plain, of average quality, with an emphasis on functionality. In their present form, most of the pieces date from the sixteenth and seventeenth centuries.

MF

Ethiopia on the Eve of Revolution: The Ebba Dettenberg-Weddig Collection

Ethiopian cross (Lallibella cross), *14th–15th century, copper, 10 3/8 x 5 7/8 in.*

Wicker vessel, Ethiopia, 19th–20th century, wickerwork made from dyed grasses, cowry shell-studded leather straps, 13 3/8 x 8 5/8 in.

The focus of this collection are its over two hundred crosses, of both the pendant and hand-held types, which assume an extraordinarily wide variety of forms and lend expression to the profound piety of Ethiopian Christians.

Ebba Dettenberg-Weddig's interests lay mainly in arts and crafts and in the Christian traditions of Ethiopia. Her collection contains utensils of everyday rural and urban life. Made using traditional handicraft techniques, these articles were still widely used in the 1960s.

The presentation highlights the following subjects: the household and nutrition, testiments of Christian faith, jewelry and traditional costumes, musical instruments, the arms of warriors and shepherds, offices and their holders, living and eating as well as desert and inland travel.

MF

Local History and Folk Art

Aristocratic Coaches and Fine Traveling Accessories

The stagecoach or mail coach, drawn by four strong horses and driven by the postilion with his whip and top hat, was *the* symbol of travel in earlier times. A coach of this kind in the typical yellow color can be admired in the large exhibition entitled "The Life of Travel: The Journey of Life" at Gottorf Palace. It does not date from the time of the likes of Joseph von Eichendorff with its Romantic sounds of the post horn, but was built about 1880, when a railway already linked

Armbruster Co., ***Mail Coach****, Vienna, ca. 1880. Last in use at the Neelsen Stallhalterei, a posting company in Kiel*

Rehm, ***Landau à la Carré****, Kiel, ca. 1890. Last used by Prince Henry of Prussia at his Hemmelmark estate*

city and country by means of steel tracks, by S. Hornbruster, a Viennese firm of high repute. That probably explains why this mail coach, which came from Austria to Schleswig via Kiel, was used only by aristocratic and upper middle-class amateurs as a prestigious four-horse carriage to take them to meetings in exclusive clubs, or to serve representative purposes in festive processions or as private seating at the racetrack.

Accessories for luxurious 19th-century carriages: *lantern for the left side of a carriage (left), two collapsible lanterns for candles, silver and brass*

In structure and details this coach authentically embodies the era of cross-country travel along established routes at affordable prices with regular stops at stations to change horses. Ten seats are high up on the roof, exposed to the wind and the rain. The others were in the stuffy, crowded interior of the closed coach body with its poor springs. According to a contemporary travel account, "The stifling interior was filled with smells of leather permeated with perspiration, musty horsehair, cart lubricant and a variety of other odors. The vehicle rumbled terribly and when the sun shone on the roof on top of everything else, the trip was torture."

Skilled cartwrights and smiths, as well as a growing number of industrial firms specialized in mass production, developed in the course of the nineteenth century the horse-drawn carriage into a supreme technical achievement that remained both grand and stylish. One example is the landau "*à la carré*" by Rehm company of Kiel, built about 1890 for Prince Henry of Prussia, the brother of Emperor William II, who was Commander-in-Chief of the German Baltic Fleet. He resided at Hemmelmark estate near Eckernförde and used the landau for his trips to Kiel. The elegant carriage with its pronounced body and rectangular doors (*à la carré*), to make getting in and out more comfortable, has elliptical springs and patented axles; the top can be folded down on either side and passengers can sit comfortably facing each other. Only a gentleman of the highest standing was entitled to display crowns on the lanterns and use maroon as his carriage's color.

The coach hall at Gottorf Palace combines original examples of almost all types and classes: the closed Berlin coaches, coupés and *dormeuses*, the open *vis-à-vis* and phaeton types, the sporty *char-à bancs* and "mail breaks," the American buggy and the English horse-drawn taxi known as a "hansom cab." The vehicles on display tell of their representative purposes at the aristocratic estates of Rohlstorff, Grünhaus, Wetterrade and Bredeneek, of great European cartwrights such as Henry Fite in Copenhagen, Mühlbauer in Paris and Lopez Sacharias in Madrid, and of the meandering routes along which historic coaches came to join the collection. For instance, before coming to Schleswig, a *dormeuse* dating from 1870 was a prop in the unforgettable "Sissi" films about the Austrian Empress Elizabeth. Its collector was Pieter-Jan van Tienhoven, estate manager and scion of an old Dutch family. Thanks to his knowledge of estates in the Holstein region he was able to save important items from destruction in modern times. Among his treasures that have enhanced the Schleswig-Holstein museum since 1992 are many hundreds of harnesses and decorative objects, luggage and picnic baskets of those who traveled in style, including lanterns and coach clocks, a historic portable medicine cabinet and a travel toilet in a mahogany case that can be flushed with water. *HM*

Carriole, Block Boat, Children's Games: The Local History Collections, Hesterberg

For the past one hundred years exactly, one of the precious possessions of the Schleswig-Holstein Museums Foundation has been a wooden horse-drawn carriage from the Wilstermarsch region known in old travel books and trade advertisements as a "carriole." It has two large, spoked wheels and a bucket seat attached where the shafts meet. The horse was driven from the seat, which had a splashboard attached in front of it and a luggage rack with two cast-iron brackets behind. The carriole stands out among the multitude of historic horse-drawn carriages because of its elaborate iron mounts and the intricate polychromed carvings on the backrest of the seat. This is not an everyday vehicle but a luxury item of the agrarian upper class in the rich marshlands of Schleswig-Holstein. The cartwright, smith and woodcarver who created it must have done so about 1785, as suggested by the Rococo style of the bas-relief ornament. The carriole seems to have gone out of fashion as early as the mid-nineteenth century, so there is no surviving memory of the owners or its exact function and driving properties. The light form of construction, the shifting of the center of gravity toward the front by placing the seat far in front of the axle, the wheels with a diameter of 4 feet 5 inches and "reinforced" with iron hoops with thick nail-heads were surely the best prerequisites for driving along the sandy trails, country lanes and bumpy dirt roads in a dashing manner. That is how we should picture the landed gentry or wealthy farmers, mayors or owners of mills driving to church, to a fair or to a council meeting in their carrioles. In fact, the German expression *herumkarjolen* still used today signifies an impetuous, somewhat reckless way of driving.

Only seven complete carriages of this type have been preserved in Germany, with an additional dozen or so of the beautifully designed bucket seats in museums. In the larger European context carrioles are related to the uniaxial French farmers' carts of the same name or the *corricolis* of Naples. In style they are closest to Norway's carrioles and particularly Holland's *Krompaneler sjees.* Dutch Friesland, which maintained close trade and naval ties with Schleswig-Holstein's west coast and sent dike builders, millers and dairy farmers to Dithmarschen and the "Old Country," could also have been the source of the tradition and construction techniques of the carriole. A special feature of the design is the unusually large camber of the wheels: the spokes radiate from the hub in almost a funnel shape to the rim. This type of construction ensured stability and maneuverability and prevented the mud of the marshes flung upward by the iron hoops from hitting the coachman. The astonishing diame-

Carriole, ca. 1785. Uniaxial touring cart of wealthy marshland farmers

ter of the wheels even made it possible to travel cross-country, over ridges and across the ditches typical of the west-coast marshlands.

Gottorf's impressive carriole is the star of the large permanent exhibition "Historic Rural Vehicles." It also displays the carriages,

Original bucket set of a carriole *(view from behind). The ornate carvings represent an allegory of the four seasons*

wagons and carts of the farmers, artisans and merchants, both robust structures made by rural cartwrights and early assembly-line products of carriage factories in Altona, Kiel and Eutin. The vehicles reflect a multitude of trades: timber wagons pulled by oxen, low wagons for transporting potable water to the pastures, the whole array of market and merchants' carts (for bakers, butchers, livestock dealers), two-wheeled dog carts for milk cans and the last surviving, massive brewer's dray used by the Eiche Brewery of Kiel. Featuring cast-iron wheels and a spring-suspended coach box, such vehicles would deliver the brewery's barrels of the beer destined to lubricate the thirsty throats of Kiel's shipyard workers every morning into the early postwar years. The master saddler Claus F. Mordhorst of Kiel made the tack for the four-horse vehicle preserved in the museum. The older citizens of Schleswig-Holstein's capital can still remember the names of the gray horses: Löwenherz (Lionheart), Marion, Hela, Fähnrich (Midshipman).

Another section is devoted to selected aspects of the joys and sorrows of travel. Visitors may admire an early nineteenth-century *Kürwagen* (bathing cart), a rack wagon with suspended seats typical of the Angeln district, a "Gettorfer" market cart popular about 1900 made by the Heinrich Brooks firm of carriage makers in Gettorf and the hunting and stalking cart used by Holstein's landed gentry. The oldest traveling coach in this large collection, a *barouchette* that still has iron C-springs and leather hangers, comes from the Goddersdorf estate. The design, fittings, including a removable *coupé*, as well as the year of construction (probably about 1780) are strikingly similar to those of the coach owned by Johann Wolfgang von Goethe that can still be admired at the poet's house in Weimar. The museum in Schleswig displays the Goddersdorf *barouchette* within the framework of an installation that tells of a rough journey on bad roads, a broken wheel and the passengers waiting for the wheelwright from the nearest village to repair it.

A special piece is Schleswig-Holstein's sole remaining bathing cart. It used to serve as a mobile changing room on the North Sea island of Föhr and was pulled far out into the water by a pair of horses to allow ladies wishing to swim to be shielded from the eyes of the male guests at the spa. These curious vehicles were a typical feature of North Sea and Baltic beaches in the nineteenth century; it was only when it became acceptable in the spas for men and women to swim together that such bathing carts lost their "moral" role.

Finally, rural funeral wagons and a wagon used for a trek from Karlsthal in Pomerania recall a past of death and hardship. In the olden days one paid one's last respects to the dead by accompanying the open black wagon carrying the coffin from the house where the deceased had died to the cemetery. On the back, carved into the wood, are the comforting words: "Do not cry; we will meet again."

Barouchette, Goddersdorf estate, Holstein, 1780. Driving over unpaved country roads caused this broken wheel

The small, authentically equipped rack wagon with a canvas cover was used on a four-week trek to flee from the approaching Red Army tanks to the safety of Schleswig-Holstein. The wife of the farmer who led the trek, Elsa Lange, who kept the wagon for decades, now shares her memories with museum visitors. The diverse vehicles, supplemented by special collections on the cartwright's and blacksmith's trades, sleighs and bicycles, are housed in a former granary. A Prussian-style brick building erected in 1870, it served the cavalry garrison stationed in Gottorf as a place to store food and feed.

Hesterberg, a "hill" only half a mile from the palace, is closely related historically and architecturally to the museum island and its complex of buildings. A second brick hall, formerly the feed barn of the Prussian cavalry, is devoted to "Fishing on the Baltic Sea." The historic fishing boats document different working and living environments. The oldest is a block boat (*Blockkahn*) from the fishing village of Gothmund near Lübeck. Built like a much older prototype in Mölln in 1926, it served the master fisher Hans Jürgen Hinrich Witt (1873–1962) as his little boat (*Lüttkahn*) for rod and line as well as trap fishing in the Trave River for precisely forty years. Characteristic of this type of boat are the stempost and sternpost made of a single oak block each, joined together by floor and side planks. The "GOT 35" boat has three areas: boxes of food supplies and fishermen's clothing are kept in the fore-ship; the mid-ship, which can be flooded separately, keeps the catch fresh; and a bench, the steering gear and a 4 hp motor are aft. Most of the time, however, the master fisher used the sail or stood up and pushed the boat along with the oar.

Surrounding Hinrich Witt's block boat are traps, landing nets and eel nets, tubs for holding fishing lines and the original tent to shelter the fishermen when they stayed overnight on the riverbank. Another display demonstrates the wide variety of nets that were used for seining and *Striekup* fishing. It includes the slim rowboat used by the fishermen of Holm, Schleswig's historic fishing settlement on the Schlei inlet. Built about 1945 in Arnis, "Schle 47" was used by the fisherman Johann Fischer for setting ledger tackle, eel traps and fixed nets. A characteristic feature of the boat is a fixed sword taking the place of a keel. Also associated with Holm and the Schlei is ice-fishing, which is illustrated in the exhibition hall with sleighs, nets, ice pick and winches. In extremely cold winters when the river froze over, all the fishermen went out on the ice and lowered a huge net through a ring of holes in the ice. With combined forces they dragged it across the fishing ground and pulled it out again. The catch, usually substantial, was distributed among all the families, including the widows of fishermen who had died at sea.

The third impressive boat in the exhibition comes from Ellerbek, a fishing village near Kiel that used to be famous far and wide. From 1870 on it had to make way for imperial plans to set up the naval base of Germany's fleet here of all places. The boat inscribed "KIE 8" and with the yellow line below the edge typical for Ellerbek was built about 1920 by the Glasau shipyard in Eckernförde. It was also on boats of this kind that the fishermen's wives, who long continued to dress in their traditional costumes, brought the catch to town. Other subjects of the exhibition are also associated with Ellerbek: smoked fish, fishmongers and the famous *Kieler Sprotten* (smoked sprats),

Three boats from important fishing communities in Schleswig-Holstein (from left to right): Ellerbek near Kiel, Schleswig's Holm on the Schlei and Gothmund near Lübeck

whose golden color comes from being smoked over a log fire. Traditionally packed in small boxes made from thin strips of wood, they were exported all over the world.

The third building on the Hesterberg housing local history collections is devoted to the world of children. It shows a selection of games and toys of the past: homemade rustic toys (a pig's bladder used as a ball, an autumnal paper kite), well-known brands of early mechanical building sets, historic board games and crafts, and lovable dolls dating from the Biedermeier to the postwar period. The focus is on the simple games and toys once popular in rural Schleswig-Holstein: *Goosschwaller*, for instance, were babies' rattles made from the gullet of a goose bent into a ring, filled with pebbles, the ends tucked into each other and then dried. *Pickpahl* is the name of a boys' game that involved hurling one's own short blackthorn stick (the *Pickpahl*) with great force into the damp ground while crowding out those of the opponents. The oldest kinds of die used by mankind are also on display: goats' or sheeps' ankle joints, the variously shaped six sides of the bones standing for the numbers one to six.

The overall theme is the difference between the girls' and the boys' worlds of play in previous centuries. Playing with their tin cranes and steam engines or waging war with plastic soldiers, the boys could dream about future careers as engineers or commanders, whereas the girls playing in the doll's house prepared for their future roles as mothers and homemakers. The precious dolls of the first third of the nineteenth century wearing original dresses imitating every detail of grownups' fashions served one purpose, namely that of preparing girls (i.e., future mothers) through play for dressing and undressing their future children. Replicas of historic toys allow young and old museum visitors to try out this role-playing and to decide for themselves whether gender-specific clichés have yet been overcome.

A particularly charming display on the Hesterberg is the museum garden presenting "Urban Horticulture around 1900." Bound by the traditional cast-iron fence and complete with an Old-Schleswig-style garden house, it shows the sensible combination of flowers and ornamental plants, vegetables and herbs. The boxwood borders around the beds recall the classic arrangement of monastery gardens. The espalier fruit trees on the south-facing brick wall are also a characteristic feature. Porcelain labels document the wide variety of both typical and almost extinct species, such as roses that are now rare, the golden European wallflower, dame's rocket or violet and the so-called eternity flower. The legendary Madonna lily, decorating many a medieval panel painting depicting the life of the Virgin, blooms only briefly, in early summer. *HM*

The Image of Popular Culture: The Folk Art Department at Gottorf Palace

The painter Jacob Alberts provides a glimpse into the well-appointed room of a house on the Hallig Hooge. His oil painting *Königspesel* of 1892 combines all the elements that, according to late nineteenth-century Romantic notions, belonged in farmhouse parlors in north Friesland: the bed in the alcove with a woven curtain, the two-room stove of ornamental cast iron with its shining warmer-shelf, the tiles decorated with marine motifs, right down to the two residents in typical regional dress. Pictures of the life of the common people by such painters as Alberts or Carl Ludwig Jessen are not photographically accurate records of everyday scenes or a certain decor. Instead they often combine objects and people from different sources in one pleasing view that corresponds with the period's ideal concept of rural life.

Comparable interiors can be seen in three-dimensional reality at Gottorf Palace's Folk Art Department. Six complete eighteenth- and nineteenth-century living rooms show furnishings and interior design from north Friesland, Holstein and Dithmarschen. One is the "Döns" (main room) of Dorn's farmstead in Dingen. This representatively appointed living room was next to the kitchen and could be heated by the "Beileger" (or "Bilegger" in local dialect) stove in the wall between the two rooms. The paneling and the wooden ceiling

*Jacob Alberts, **Königspesel**, 1892, oil on canvas, 31 ½ x 39 ¼ in.*

Mangle boards from the Wilstermarsch, second half 18th century, 26 1/8 x 5 7/8 in. and 24 x 6 3/4 in.

painted with biblical scenes are dated 1800 but hark back to the formal idiom of the Baroque. Complete rooms such as this have been assembled and shown in northern and central European museums since the nineteenth century. The pieces of furniture do not all come from one house. If the original stove, seat-furniture or table were missing, for instance, objects from other provenances were added.

The Yacht "The Woman Katharina Schiffer" of Captain Lorenz Peter Carben in Flensburg, 1823, captain's picture, pen and ink, wash, 15 ¼ x 20 ⅝ in.

The Schleswig-Holstein rooms shown here were subject to additional changes after 1945, when they were moved from the Thaulow Museum in Kiel that had been destroyed in the war to the new museum at Gottorf Palace.

Chests, wardrobes, jewelry and clothing add to our picture of the different regions of preindustrial Schleswig-Holstein. Of its substantial holdings of ornamental and utility items, the museum's Folk Art Department displays the most skillfully made ones. Everyday objects were made to serve a purpose and were decorated very simply, such as the museum's wooden mangle boards, which were used to smooth out the damp laundry after it had been wrapped around a wooden roll. However, there are also some particularly elaborately carved and painted boards from regions in the German-speaking part of the area. The museum shows examples from the Wilstermarsch and north Friesland made by local carpenters or woodcarvers. They are often inscribed with a date and dedications or monograms. The Wilstermarsch mangle boards bear motifs and ornaments of Baroque courtly art, such as amorous couples and garlands of flowers and fruit. Decorative elements in the classical style are also in evidence, such as acanthus vines, as are allegories, such as the personification of Christian Charity (*caritas*, i.e., love) as a woman with two children. The colorfully painted boards were most likely gifts. They were presumably never used to smooth linen, for they show no signs of use.

Similarly, the colorfully painted ceramics manufactured by Schleswig-Holstein factories in Kellinghusen and the Probstei were merely showpieces. Earthenware with a lead glaze had been manu-

***Scottish hunter**, Staffordshire, ca. 1860, faience, $17\frac{3}{4} \times 9\frac{1}{2} \times 2\frac{3}{4}$ in.*

factured in the Probstei, the area around the Preetz Monastery south of Kiel, since the mid-eighteenth century. The production of plates, tureens, drinking vessels and vases in pewter-glazed faience began in several factories in Kellinghusen at about the same time. The Kellinghusen faience dishes shown in the Folk Art Department are examples of the mass-produced, low-price wares manufactured in the nineteenth century as a consequence of growing competition in industrially made ceramics. It is interesting to compare them to the early Baltic faience shown in the Rococo Department (see pp. 53–58), which includes early Kellinghusen products. They had been destined mainly for aristocratic and upper middle-class customers, whereas the buyers of Probstei and Kellinghusen ceramics were the well-to-do rural population.

Life in the area of today's Schleswig-Holstein was always determined by its position "between the seas." The great importance of seafaring is illustrated in the Folk Art Department by various utensils, works of art and souvenirs: nautical instruments, objects made from carved walrus teeth (scrimshaw) and the so-called captains' pictures. Captains used to have precise depictions of their ships, including every detail of the superstructure and rigging, made by specialized painters. This type of commemorative picture has existed since the eighteenth century in almost all coastal regions of Europe. Today the paintings are important documents of historic sailing vessels.

Seafarers' souvenirs include earthenware figures made in the English county of Staffordshire. Often bought by sailors as small gifts, though mainly imported in large quantities via the usual trade routes, these products were very popular in what is now Schleswig-Holstein. Besides the famous pairs of dogs, the Staffordshire pugs, still manufactured in large quantities today, other Staffordshire products made their way to the north of Germany from the eighteenth century on: clock cases, flower vases and above all ornamental figures, including portraits of famous generals, actresses and members of the nobility. Because of their usual location, they were called "chimney ornaments." In the nineteenth century, in response to Romantic sympathy with the struggle for Scottish liberation, the fashion was for figures of Scots, as shown in the museum: anonymous Scotsmen in kilts, Scots folk heroes and members of the ruling family. Staffordshire figures with their white glaze, painted decoration in bright colors and low prices were also popular decorative items throughout northern Germany.

Joining the decorative and aesthetic displays of the Folk Art Department are the utensils and jewelry, interiors, furniture and clothing from various regions of Schleswig-Holstein, in several rooms on the mezzanine. They are displayed according to the nineteenth-century concept of museums of art and design, which was to show outstanding examples as prototypes for contemporary craftsmen. *BK*

Museum Branches

Museum of Cast Iron, Büdelsdorf

The neoclassical platter cast about 1820 by the Royal Prussian Foundry in Berlin is one of the outstanding achievements of Prussian casting. The central ornament and the outer frieze are both modeled on the art of classical antiquity: the gorgon's head on the Medusa Rondanini kept in Munich's Glyptothek and the frieze on the temple of Apollo at Bassae. The Greek frieze had been excavated in 1812 and taken to the British Museum in London in 1815. Reproductions of it spread rapidly and the Royal Academy of Art in Berlin acquired a plaster cast in 1818. It shows battles between Amazons and Greeks, Lapiths and Centaurs. The platter's inner frieze depicts winged goddesses of victory and classicizing garlands.

The cast-iron jewelry, small utensils, furniture and furnishings such as those presented in two sections of this museum were quite

Royal Prussian Foundry, Berlin, ***platter bearing a depiction of the Medusa Rondanini****, ca. 1820, cast iron, diam. 16 ½ in.*

common in the nineteenth century. The early beginnings of the technique are illustrated by Far Eastern examples. Another section covers the "Carlshütte," the foundry established by Marcus Hartwig Holler in Büdelsdorf in 1827. Käthe Ahlmann, a descendent of the family who continued to run the foundry into the twentieth century, assembled a collection covering far more than their own products. It includes cast-iron sculpture, medals and bas-reliefs of the nineteenth century. In addition, numerous cast-iron fireplace and stove plates, "Beileger" and pyramid stoves dating from 1500 to 1840 bear witness to the importance of cast iron through the centuries. Examples of modern cast iron round off the comprehensive exhibition.

Eisenkunstguss-Museum, Glück-Auf-Allee 4, 24782 Büdelsdorf, (04331) 387 11

Jewish Museum, Rendsburg

The portrait of Genia Fürstenberg, much admired by the artist Max Liebermann, corresponds in two senses to the nature of this museum run by the Schleswig-Holstein Museums Foundation: both artist and sitter were Jewish and suffered under the persecution of the Jews by the National Socialists. The sitter was the wife of the banker Hans (Jean) Fürstenberg, son of Carl Fürstenberg, Senior Managing Director of the Berlin Trading Company. When the couple had to emigrate to Switzerland, they took the painting with them.

The full-length portrait depicts Genia Fürstenberg to stunning effect. Wearing a black evening gown and a marceled 1920s-style hairdo, she is seated on a sofa in an extremely elegant pose. Her right arm rests on the armrest, tracing its curve in a lovely, sweeping line. The delicate shawl draped over it emphasizes the bend of her arm and the glowing skin through the precious material. In an equally graceful gesture, her left arm stretches out on a shimmering, green silk cushion. Her crossed legs and the flowing fabric of her filmy gown taper toward the bottom in a sweeping, elegant line.

Besides the work of Max Liebermann, that of other Jewish artists is also represented here. Included are paintings by Felix Nussbaum dating from his exile in Belgium, the portrait by Rudolf Levy of Serge Lifar, a dancer in the Ballets Russes, and portraits by Ludwig Meidner. Meidner was able to escape to England, returning to Germany later, whereas Nussbaum was murdered in Auschwitz and Levy presumably died while being deported to a concentration camp.

The Talmud Torah school and the former synagogue constitute the Jewish Museum. The synagogue also features a ritual bath (*mikvah*) in the cellar. Exhibited along with works by Jewish and German

Max Liebermann (1847–1935), ***Genia Fürstenberg,*** *ca. 1924–25, oil on canvas, 78 ¾ x 48 in.*

artists are religious implements and documentation on the history of Jews in Schleswig-Holstein.

The Jewish Museum also holds temporary exhibitions on contemporary art and subjects related to Jewish history and culture in the large hall and on the former women's gallery of the synagogue. The Julius Magnus House provides additional space for temporary exhibitions and documentation.

Jüdisches Museum, Prinzessinstrasse 7–8, 24768 Rendsburg, (04331) 252 62

Founded in the thirteenth century, this Benedictine monastery was renovated in the eighteenth. In the west wing a modern hall on the ground floor, Rococo rooms on the second and a Gothic hall on the third are used for temporary exhibitions today. Of the original buildings, only the church and the cellar with the well have been preserved. The church has one of the oldest known altarpieces, built as a reliquary shrine shortly after 1300. The original painted decoration of the bas-relief carvings is almost completely preserved. In the cellar housing the well there is documentation on the history and use of the building.

Kloster Cismar, Bäderstrasse 42, 23743 Cismar, (04366) 10 80

BR

*The vaulted hall on the second floor of **Cismar Monastery**, today used for temporary exhibitions*

New Departures, Perspectives and Visions

Can splendid scenarios that occurred as long as 350 years ago be repeated? Do glorious historic epochs have inspiring, long-term effects that allow them to re-establish themselves? Looking at Gottorf Palace at the turn of the twenty-first century gives the impression that the abundant springs of the past, after being blocked for many years, have been made to flow again. It even seems that the completely new framework of the museum foundation implanted in the palace has reactivated them.

Supposing that the proposal to release the museums from government control, in order to permit an independent kind of cultural activity oriented on economic parameters, is really meant seriously. Supposing that the subsidies from public funds continue to be guaranteed and that they rise adequately in relation to the cost of living so that museum authorities need not tremble from one budget to the next. Then merging the museums in the foundation—despite the nonexistent capital—could set free positive energies. Above all, working on a commercial basis could bring about—whether or not anticipated in policy, planned or deliberately contemplated—the revival of the seventeenth-century Gottorf *Kunstkammer* in the twenty-first century. This means the productive collaboration of active museum work with scholarly research on a period spanning the prehistory of humankind to the present day. Anyone who can make centuries-old stones "speak" and try to cross them with contemporary works of art, who can make the interdisciplinary network of weather-dependent tourism, the interested general public and specialists in art and cultural history, including archaeology and ethnology, into an exciting experience has managed to bring about constellations similar to those at work in the Golden Age of Gottorf's Baroque era, but under completely different circumstances.

The seventeenth-century dukes of Gottorf, Frederick III and Christian Albert, created a fascinating synthesis of enthusiasm for the arts, thirst for cultural and historical knowledge, and scientific curiosity in the palace, the Baroque garden with its cosmological symbolism, the Giant Globe that was a technical and scientific wonder, the *Kunstkammer* and the library that reflected the most up-to-date knowledge of the then-known world. In both art *and* science their court scholar Adam Olearius transcended the courtly world of Gottorf in exemplary fashion. His unusual voyage as an envoy to Moscow and Persia from November 1633 to August 1639 and the description of his travels, translated into several languages, opened a window on the world.

Christian Rothgiesser, Adam Olearius, ca. 1655, engraving, 6 ⅜ x 4 ⅛ in. In English translation the Latin inscriptions read: in the oval frame: "Adam Olearius from Aschersleben in Saxony, librarian and mathematician at the Schleswig-Holstein court at fifty-five years of age"; directly beneath the portrait: "Thou shalt guide me with thy counsel, And afterward receive me to glory" (Psalm 73:24); below appear the words of the jurist Polycarp Wirth from Leipzig: "Whoever you are, cast your gaze hither; look, my [friend] Olearius is showing you his visage, with which the ruler of the Russians deigned to become acquainted and the ruler of Persia, rich in Sufi incense. Since he could not be depicted in heaven, as befitted his spirit, he proffered himself, that it may be recognized in his spirit."

International experience liberated local ideas and, in turn, Gottorf's luminosity was brought to European awareness. Olearius's research thrived on the "not yet but surely yes" typical of the changing times. Things that could be observed began to be investigated and probed scientifically, yet they continued to be seen as an "ingenious game" of nature (Olearius). There was no doubt that everything that people admired, particularly the curios from the past collected and available for analysis at Gottorf from this period on, was created by God. The perception of the world as God's work was unshakable. But this creation was subject to every line of inquiry imaginable. And this is what represents the progress and the breakthroughs achieved by Adam Olearius as he inspired his dukes. In the grand design of the globe, which could fit twelve people in its interior, he captured the macrocosm in the microcosm. With the world on the outside and the view of the heavens inside, it conjured up predictable interrelationships.

The psychology of the Giant Globe's success at the time and its continuing widespread appeal among specialist circles to this day—when the decision in 2000 to rebuild Gottorf's Globe was announced, all kinds of spontaneous support was demonstrated—motivates the Schleswig-Holstein Museums not to lay on the pathos of remembrance, but to see the history of art and culture in the light of the intellectually open-minded history of the palace. The striking diversity of the museums' collections can thus serve to provide an enriching encounter and stabilizing roots for the foundation's public.

HG

Opposite: The west wing of Gottorf Palace and the northwestern corner tower

Photographic Acknowledgments

Gisela Floto: front and back cover images, pp. 2, 5–6, 12–13, 14, 15, 40, 41, 189
All other photographs provided by the Stiftung Schleswig-Holsteinische Landesmuseen Schloss Gottorf

Detail of Baroque organ front dating from ca. 1567